LOVE ITSELF

LOVE ITSELF
IN THE LETTER BOX

BY HÉLÈNE CIXOUS

TRANSLATED BY PEGGY KAMUF

polity

First published in French as *L'amour même dans la boîte aux lettres* by
Hélène Cixous © Editions Galilée, 2005

This English edition © Polity Press, 2008

Polity Press
65 Bridge Street
Cambridge CB2 1UR, UK

Polity Press
350 Main Street
Malden, MA 02148, USA

ISBN-13: 978-07456-3988-8
ISBN-13: 978-07456-3989-5 (pb)

A catalogue record for this book is available from the British Library.

Typeset in 10.75 on 14 pt Adobe Janson by Servis Filmsetting Ltd,
Stockport, Cheshire
Printed and bound in Great Britain by Biddles Ltd, King's Lynn, Norfolk

For further information on Polity, visit our website: www.polity.co.uk

Ouvrage publié avec le concours du Ministére français chargé de la culture –
Centre National du Livre.

Published with the assistance of the French Ministry of Culture –
National Centre of the Book

CONTENTS

I

OLIVIER DE SERRES

– A SINGLE PASSION

TWO WITNESSES

I passed in front of Olivier de Serres which saddens me you say I try to recapture exact details in the flesh but I can't picture the place remains the same you say,

The scene-that-remains one day you were returning from vacation I fell upon you we made love on the floor I remember the texture of your skin you say which saddens me remains the texture

we are sitting on The Divan all of a sudden we fall upon the scene-that-remains, I lean over I see you fall all of a sudden on her me who I was, it is there! this brilliant scene returned to fall in front of us, it/she is on the floor on the carpet, it/she is on your face, I see us on your face look at us falling all of a sudden, there. I thought, I remember: thus, he returns – thus he has come out of disappearance, he has returned from his non-returning – I remember I thought: all is well, I sinned, I didn't believe and god is the unbelievable, I thought: thus he returns, the one who will never return, at that moment the thing (of) my soul fell into the height of the sky, you throw a little pebble into the sky and that's me

I am afraid of you and I fear you I abandon myself by not expecting you each time that you return I'm knocked over backwards by it you have me falling at your feet, I thought, struck by lightning I thought all the same, I have always thought under lightning, then you gave me a reed, a kind of stylus pen while saying to me "I wasn't expecting 'that'" you were not forewarned of this return, I say – which return? you say – yours I say

You don't remember what precedes never, I thought, sitting, on The Divan, always on your right flank, our knees rubbing lightly against each other, but I say nothing to you, I look at you look at us fall in the scene-that-remains, your lips suck the sugared flow of the thing that happened that comes back up always by way of the mouth, comes to lick the tongue and reawaken words, I look at your lips, you suck at memory's nipple, "the two witnesses" I say to myself, we are the two witnesses of ourselves, the two witnesses of the scene-that-remains, not bearing the same witness, a single scene makes for two scenes.

– Then you gave me a reed, that is to say a pen.

– Me? I gave you a pen?

– It's a metaphor I say. I said to you: no one will ever write the taste of this scene, and you said to me, "give me something to eat, now."

I was always afraid that my mother would suddenly enter.

Or, in order, my son, then my daughter.

There are seven fears at the doors and windows of my life, and a terror that fills my chest and entrails, that's you.

To come back to the two witnesses. There was no place more like a temple than Olivier de Serres, a dark and necessary little studio. Temples are places that spend their time trembling, splitting apart and caving in, catching fire, collapsing, rising back up and their foreheads are touched by the wings of jackdaws that howl postprophetically: they see misfortunes coming only after the fact

– Rise and measure the Temple as a *remainder*, you say
– As I recall, it could not have been larger than 15 m².

When struggles take place in a small room they are all the more terrible, one is in a grotto, a cellar, a cell, a hut the walls are crumbling, they show traces of soot, Olivier de Serres was tiny, a hole in a dead-end street, with some English furniture. That's where we prophesized, mouth to mouth, you bite me, it's always you who bite, bite, bite, I didn't dare. On my side I drank I swallowed your book, in my mouth it had the sweetness of honey, but right afterwards my entrails were bitter because I was jealous of my own mouth. It swallows everything and keeps nothing I thought. But I never dared say to you: I want to swallow your sperm and keep it outside me at the same time. My too little my everything my not enough.

To come back to the two witnesses. The two restorer-demolisher heroes of the Temple, tenants of Eternity for a few hours, those of whom it is said: "These are *the two olive trees* and the two torches *standing before the Lord of the earth*" who are they? Who are we? We are Thursday, February 12, 2005.

People have spoken of Moses and Elijah, Peter and Paul. Names. And we?

We, the names, we left them outside right away. We call ourselves: you, or else we. You, you, and we. Each time I say: we, I am afraid, I fear you and I fear fate. Who can swear to "we"? No one. "We," I say timidly and imprudently and I scrutinize your face to see if it's OK.

In forty years, on average forty times a year, that makes one thousand six hundred control checks.

– You remember? you say.

– Yes, I say, I believe so. I'm recalling this moment I remember it living, hastily, I bite into it, it's February 12, 2005, blue sweater, gray shoes, 4:30 in the afternoon, themes: "solitudes" "invention," "the last time," the-last-time-that-we-the-first-

time-that-we-thought-or-said-explicitly "it's-the-last-time,"
I remember this moment, brief shelter of time, we are sitting
on the divan and I recall that we are sitting on the divan at that
moment you lay your head once more on my right shoulder,
remember this instant I say to myself, a supply of joy for sev-
eral days. Meanwhile I recall with you I believe, I believe
I know what recalls itself to you, this very little scene, it's our
child and our childhood, it would be terrible if we had for-
gotten it, it would be infanticide, at the time we didn't know
that we had conceived a tenuous but very powerful child, we
bent down over her, over him, over the photo, there I say in
this moment, you have the same empty look that Abraham had
when he looks at Isaac for the last time: the texture of his skin.
That's already a lot for memory, it's already the essential.

 – You remember what? I say.

 – It was the end of a summer you were returning I threw
myself upon you, I will never forget this is the first time that
I tell you this memory, you say.

Each time it/she returns to him, it's the first time, the mys-
tery of this scene is its power to return to him each time for
the first time

I never say that this scene has already taken place, the scene
where he remembers the memory of childhood for the first
time, that's the charm, his charm and that of the scene.

It returns every three years, for the first time it must have a
secret periodic rhythm.

Little by little this scene, the unique one, and its scene of rep-
etition take on a grandeur, little by little the scene and its second
time are elevated to the sacred. Repetition adorns it with adora-
tion. The little scene is now one of the greatest scenes in our book

I never say: you told it to me, remember, in the Japanese
restaurant. Never! That would be our suicide. I want the
springtime. I admire it. It returns each time trembling all over
from having crossed cemeteries.

It is the fairy or the feast. We contemplate it in silence as it passes by, brief and blazing ceremony. We fall, sometimes on the ground, sometimes on the carpet, sometimes with eyes wide open as if fascinated sometimes in an expiration
– So you see? We are still there, we say to Someone. In my view it is to Death that we say that, but we do not grant it the name.

The Scene grows.

Something very important must have happened that day the first one, the ancient one. When it comes back, this scene, it is always glorious. This thing must have always returned from among the dead. "Impossible not to live," it says. It has tried. In vain. It grows.

I never recall it. You are its guardian and its narrator. You bring it back to me.

On April 14, 2004, when the scene suddenly made one of its apparitions, you added a detail to it. We were seated on the divan as usual, you placed your right hand on my left knee. The scene made its entrance.

We made love on the floor.

We made love with this scene.

I never recall any of our scenes with my words. It's you the captain, the head of speech. I do not speak the words I'm thinking of, they remain in the streets, in the airports, in the train stations, phantoms uneasy about their fate. No one will ever know them. I do not dare to give them the right to see the day.

And if you didn't remember them? They would die.

You can forget or not forget, I don't want to exercise over you the right of evocation.

– Let me do it, I'm the head.

– You're the head of *forget-and-remember*. My memory is not as valiant as yours. But I live in my memory. Our memory has two memories. Our memory has two forgettings. You come into my hut. I go into your memory. Each one at home at the other's

"I let you do it, I let myself be led along I let you make me me I say, as much as it can be done and as possible as it is possible to will – but not always."

All of a sudden I reread all the Bibles, I go, I come, I search, from one language to another I read from Bible to Bible, my Luther, your King James the old little ones, the young big ones, I pass my tongue over them again, I pace back and forth in the deserts, I find again your traces, your ancestries, I know you, I have already encountered you, I have already heard your voice, already I have not seen you, you are a summary of the desert, already I must have crossed you for forty years and it begins again. I find you look like Moses my dog you look like Abraham my cat, your speech is brief, you don't speak you let loose sentences, your poems, that's it: it barks, it spurts. And then the stone-words, the shard-words, the formulas, the capsules containing all of God.

Your language – I always come back to it – is well guarded, I try to part your lips with my tongue or else it's you on my lips, I no longer know what is inside what is outside, are your words in my mouth when I read them in your language, the slightest touch of a syllable has the mysterious power of a penetration.

– **Had I not written my poems in English, would you have loved me?**[1]

– What a question!

The whole body of this story, our longshortlife, suddenly folds up, flattens out, hollows out its back, slides itself, like a letter into a box, in a hut where our memory of childhood shines beneath the dust.

---

[1] Bold characters indicate here, and throughout, English used in the original. (Tr)

The Memory is succinct in lively colors, it comes back alive
from the other world when all memories have for so long gone
back to sleep. A fugitive dream that looks for a corner in which
to settle.

No one knows why certain memories come back alive,
others half dead.

You threw yourself upon me as if I had turned round on you
as if I had opened a small gap in your thigh, as if you had
become convinced that I wanted to devour you like a panther
behaving like a real person, which I would never have thought
of doing for anything in the world, but overturning the fore-
sight of what it seemed should never be, this moment resem-
bling a dream and yet bearing a powerful reality.

Who could have told me that everything that seemed
incredible at Olivier de Serres when we were down there as if
knocked over and trampled beneath paws, now forty years
later we ourselves would look upon from above like gods look-
ing at the affairs of mortals? And subsequently, when the days
in which we are will in turn be part of the past, where? who?
seized by a fearful admiration? will we be? our two witnesses?
Or like gods watching from the next mountain these two that
we will then have been?

When I evoke Olivier de Serres following your lead, I am
in the midst of reading *Demeure, Athènes* the strange twice-
haunted text by Derrida: haunted once by the death of
Socrates who is a beautiful woman, dressed in white, beauti-
ful as her name tall as her soul dressed in daylight, more
exactly in the hour of the day's dawning, a second time in truth
perhaps the first, by a sentence. This sentence is also tall and
beautiful, but for its part or for her part, she does not come,
she precedes everyone:

the text, the narrative, the reading, the author, the actors, the witnesses, she, this sentence, is there before us, when I talk to you about it you too you shiver, you tell me that she is not unknown to you, you have already found yourself in front of her, but as for you, you do not think she is beautiful but hard and authoritarian

"*Nous nous devons à la mort*," "We owe ourselves/each other to death," it says, she says. The voice is metallic, you say. Whereas I find this voice elastic like the air of a cat acquiescing to the laws of Nature.

How different we are I thought: the same words say things otherwise to us.

The two non-identifiable feminine characters the woman in white and the sentence in the blank, monotone voice give rendezvous to the two heroes, Jacques Derrida and Socrates.

And that, I will never do, *give you a rendezvous*. That is indeed a perfidious, dreadful expression. A rendezvous to you, *à toi*? Never.

The convocation of the two men: their indictment, their conviction, and what is their crime? Life.

And to say that the two feminine characters are so beautiful and so indifferent.

The thrice-beautiful woman, by the way they speak of her I feel they are under her spell, if I were I man I would recognize her, I would be a little bald in appearance but my mouth would be open on a heart-shaped tongue, I would chuckle in delight, my eyes would split apart in the middle of my cheeks for my whole body would be lifted by the voice of my mother, the inedible nourishing dew. And what song does she sing, what song did she sing beforever? "I am life." "My baby my darling my nursling do not fear mama life is here. Every hour I give you is good." Do not fear says the sentence. It's a marvelous text that makes me weep the kind of warm tears that surprise me each time I think I see a weeping child who believes he or she is abandoned.

– I am going to be jealous – Of whom? – Of Jacques
Derrida. Of Socrates. One after the other, one theme after the
other, life, death.

It's not easy what I am confiding to you here as if to myself,
it's made of extreme joy that in the end is sad but without pain.

In the end one always needs one's mother so as to be born
on the other side.

– I will always be there, I will say to you, the next time. Even
after the door. It's neither a gift nor a promise. It's a natural
phenomenon. As durable but no more so than a mountain.
You can climb on me for millions of years. I am stable, etched
by ravines, immobile, torn and flooded by torrential springs.

I am no more beautiful than I am. On occasion I give up or
almost. There was, in the new house that we just bought and
which I have not yet even inspected altogether, the morning
of our first night, the baby left here by my youngest daughter.
It was a baby external to me. When it began to cry in the early
morning, I let it cry I had other things to do. All the moving
house. Until the moment I saw the little face turn to mush, just
like a potato wrinkled by sorrow. Poor thing. So, I picked it
up. Its little limbs stuck to my skin, and the baby began to
make up part of my body, so I took it into the kitchen to give
it some milk. I confess: the *trust* came first from it, it was the
baby who took me in its four limbs and filled me with trust.
The mother sometimes is the child.

I am not confiding secrets in you. All things are decided and
applied by very powerful events lost today in a *forgotten for-
getting*, one hasn't any trace of them, but our acts obey. All our
acts of faithfulness as of unfaithfulness are commanded by
Causes. We don't know them but it is not impossible that they
will be revealed to us, one day, suddenly, often very late, in his-
tory's story, one has to count on a delay of at least forty-five or
fifty years.

I barely knew this child. Between us there had been no

time. When I picked it up it spread throughout my blood in my flesh, at maddening speed, and in a minute it had been in my story forever.

When you fell on me I became a mountain from then on. There had already been a first time. But that was then one time. The time becomes the first only with the second time. The time that was not yet the first, I did not become a mountain. That was in New York in your office. Time: prehistory. One afternoon without expectation without memory without premonition. Without appearance. At least in appearance.

All the times that are destined to become first times are the same in all books. One sees nothing coming. One sees no one. Suddenly it explodes. People whom one did not see enter shove you so hard from behind, some might call them angels, external powers yet who? There is no seduction. You remember nothing and you come to, wounded knowing not where, survivors, a tenth of the city has toppled, beneath the ruins you feel your body you feel the wrong body, you can't do otherwise. You come to. You excuse yourselves. There is no explanation.

You give me Artaud's letters to Genica Athanasiou
 – Why do you do that? The next day?
 – The next day?
 – After. It's a next day, a tomorrow. – The too morrow? – All words open up under the shock, I remember. Each word from your mouth. You say tomorrow in French, *demain*. I look at your *deux mains*, your two hands. I see them. It's the first part of you I see. After, I stop.
 – You saw me I say?
We are in 2004. We have come back. Today I can ask you: you saw me?
 – You mean? Saw? In what sense? At what moment? No. The first time I saw you I did not see you.
 – In the end, I say, I looked at your hands. I wasn't seeing you

Your body, that's a word I would not have said. I clung to your hands so that something human might exist in the chaos. – What does it mean to say to see? What does to see mean to say? you say. Saturday, June 18, 2004. All words began to say and most of them were saying: No. The next day you put the letters from A. to G. A. in my letter box.

– I did that?

– You put these letters to me. Look at you look at me look at that. Look at who. I would have liked not to believe you. What broke out suddenly was fire. We heard nothing coming. You give me back a collection of Celan, who is it? I say. At that moment I hear – like an inaudible Voice crying out my name, an interior Voice therefore, I recognize my father's anger: "Come up here!" I raise my leg, that is to say, I want to raise it and it's impossible; strength has gone out of my legs. I can neither go up nor go back. I take my leg in my two hands. I can't lift it.

– Your frightened emotion, you clutch at the sky with my hands as if it were falling on your head breathlessly when I kissed you. I have this image that's alive in June 2004.

– I was afraid it was irreparable. I was afraid it was reparable.

– Was he you or was he me? what did you mean to say? I ask that in June 2004.

– I was afraid you would always be there. I didn't want to tell you that earlier.

– Letters from terror to horror, *l'épouvante*.

It begins with fear. Because of absolute solitude. In New York I experienced the solitude with such violence that I felt like crouching under a café table. The poets who accompanied me, all of them phantoms, don't attack me, don't defend me. I didn't know there was someone in your office; I thought it was a library. Having read a volume of your poems I would never have thought they had a master. I could have stolen some without its being a theft.

I remember your arrival in the office. I remember the other being that you appeared to be to me then when I had just read the poems with a freedom for which you might reproach me. I had licked them from head to toe, chewed ruminated without paying, they were mine, and suddenly they were yours, they were something of your person that I had taken pleasure with behind your back I had helped myself, as if I had gone into the wrong bedroom, I slept in your bed, your dreams came to me, thereupon you enter, you turn on the light, I jump up, it's not as if I could say: I thought you were dead. I was with your poems and I had no need of you.

When I talk about New York April 14, I get the instinctive urge to reread *A Passion in the Desert*. I begin running around in all directions, there is such a need. I do not remember it at all. – Is it a novel? you say. You do not remember it at all. I remember a few cinders in a blazing fire. Bookstores don't have Passion. It increases. Like an order surging out of the Desert of Memory. One obeys. Search. Find. Taste. When I get these orders, by day or night, I always obey. Why wouldn't I obey? I obey the Great Goddess of Forgetting. If I Forgot it's because the thing was tied up with some secret that had been buried alive. A weeping calls faintly to me. It's because I must be in the Myrtle Grove, in Book VI of *The Aeneid*, when Aeneas having descended into the Inferno catches sight of the little wood where those whose harsh love has eaten away their heart with its cruel poison and whose sorrows remain alive in death are hiding. This neutral joy that orders me does not have the sweet taste of cake, but that of the fear of being at fault. The bitter taste of fear.

– How do you write *l'épouvante*? you say to me.

There is a carnage of panthers in the wood, an odor of blood and sunstruck laurel. Males or females? I don't dare look at their sex. Moreover I'm awash with tears, I relive ten times over the last hours of my beloved Thessie, the one whose pure love does not die in death, it's she her adored bodycadaver that I see dispersed tenfold in the wood, I begin to run toward all the victims, I cut locks of their fur, I weep over the white- black- and gold-colored hairs, which are now dead and will have no more rebirths, a mad avarice spurs me on, I want to keep everything, I want to lose nothing of you, not a look, not a hair, I will go with you to the barber's, I will gather up the sheared living locks, whom do I weep for, whom did I weep for, on August 30, 2001, when I wept for our unique witness, the being who watched us without blinking, with the round and profound eyes of God? What was I weeping for while kissing her consenting lips?

What was the name of Balzac's cat? She was a large and beautiful calico, he took hold of her tail so as to count its black and white rings, he spent hours contemplating the soft, refined contours, the intoxicating whiteness of the belly, the grace of the head, he admired her suppleness when she leapt crawled, when she slid, when she buried herself in him when she clung rolled when she snuggled threw herself against him everywhere, when she turned over cooing while he rubbed his hand on her nipples on her sex stretching her arms and legs to guide him toward the cleft of pleasure, when she took him in her arms so as to place her delicate rosy lips on his thick lips while he got hard when she straddled him with tender art full of genius and able therefore to feel jealousy, sinking down with eyes rolled back in pain without any restraint with the poignant non-modesty that no woman had ever shown him. If there had not been the cat on his body's earth he would never have known more than the outline of voluptuousness that ends up dissipating under caresses in a dream. When he began to worship a woman he found himself hoping she would let herself go under his skilled hands to the point of the cat but each one of them pointed him suddenly in a false direction. And this is something he was never able to say to anyone. He made many starts but soon he was alone like a shed skin. Such a thing ought to be possible all the same, he would say to himself, but I will never see the proof of it in my lifetime.

Someone whom I don't know by name whose face I don't see doubtless knows where I know nothing. An oracle. I didn't even know any longer if I had ever known who died of love in the desert, who was the Desert. In general, the Desert is God.

When finally I receive *A Passion in the Desert*, it's not a novel, it's not a story, it's –

when you have read it, in your turn, you will tell me

– it's a magic object in which the souls of our dead are kept, at once captive and preserved for the day when if we pass near enough to the tree, here a date palm, they rustle, call us asking only to be recognized so that finally the charm of forgetting might be broken

– to my stupefaction it is a savage and prophetic version of *Demeure, Athènes*

A Passion in the Desert is our error it's the costumed portrait of one of our interior tragedies, a delicate and cruel representation of one of our personal massacres, through a disfiguration of the miracle, through a mirage.

It begins with fear, passion begins with a fear. Fear is the trembling of faith. One cannot have faith without being afraid. One cannot *have* faith, no human being. Being human is that: to have faith that's been fractured then stuck back together. Being feline is the opposite. In this story there are only two persons on earth, one doesn't know if it happens before or after the existence of humanity. The two beings are each half of the house of the world. The young man is alone in a blackish space, even his voice does not reach his ears. He is ready to die, if not to live. His only friends the palm trees. He becomes a sort of palm tree that can walk. Then he lies down surrounded by the palms in the grotto, as if in the thought of death. It was a third of July, in the middle of the night the alternating accent of a savage breathing awakens him. It is a sentence. *"Nous nous devons à la mort"* says the respiration and, frozen in place, he thinks its energy cannot belong to a human creature. He rejects it with all his petrified strength. He says nothing. He is not. He hates not. He is in its power. Without knowing who has hold of him. Is it a lion, a tiger, a crocodile, rolled up like a big dog, there's a foxy odor but heavier, little by little it's a male panther, its muzzle spotted with blood, finally it's a female panther, it's Albertine wrapped in a Fortuny coat, the upper part of the yellow coat like gold matte smooth and soft bears the famous rose-shaped flecks in imitation of Carpaccio, it's too beautiful to believe, one already senses that the man is going to rise above himself higher and higher stronger and stronger to the height of God's toe, until he touches it, until he touches God's Toe with his toe and to the point of such infinitely voluptuous contact between two so terribly different species

– This silence –
– Well, so, finish the story!
The lady, to whom the gentleman, to whom the narrator related this extravagant story that Balzac tries to share with us, is telling a not-very-ordinary story, begins to get irritated. She is the one who utters this sentence.

One should go no further. One has had enough, one fears the ending, one desires it, one wants it to be over, it would be wise to possess oneself with great pleasure of this tiny infinite parcel of the absolute, the spark of happiness that flares up at the zero point of contact between the two toes without which one would have died without ever having known – but one always wants to go further to see, cease waiting in other words stop coming with pleasure.

– So – finish the story, says the lady. Neither Balzac nor the lady submit this sentence to commentary.

– "Finish the story?" says the gentleman, who is out in front of the lady. It's horribly difficult.

He's the one, the young soldier, who is afraid. The other being does not know fear. He with his greenish and darting eyes like the sea is a Saint-Loup, the other with her yellow and staring eyes like steel is an apparition. What makes him afraid is the enormity of the life that looks at him immobile. She is still but a young girl in flowers, this mighty life with yellow eyes and rosy lips. Next you will see him spend long hours in the shadow of Her Presence. There is no more time, only hours, in this ahuman realm. Morning and night the sentence returns. He becomes accustomed to it, to her. He submits to her presence. It's because she was there before him, he's the intruder in the grotto. For all eternity then she will have preceded him, and without hurrying, she will have overtaken him, with that immobile speed of big cats inhabited by leaps to come. That's why he admits that she makes advances to him. In his turn he makes advances to her.

He cannot turn around and go back. The desert does not have this.

It's during the long hours when hope abandons him that he amuses himself with the panther. During this long engagement having for image only each other, a faint metamorphosis comes over them, an intelligence, a language. And yet never will the soldier's solitude have been greater, and this growing solitude, who could have told him it was love? It's because betrayal rises up in his blood along with the heady sensation that he owes her from now on what he will never want to give her.

– "All the same, this is not going to last forever" he thinks, in French. But his caresses say the opposite.

He thinks that the being other thinks: forever.

He thinks: I want to ask Mademoiselle to leave us. He is so jealous of his freedom. But which one? Whose freedom? All of a sudden he has the anguished thought that he has advanced too far into the desert: in the solitary and burning golden sands he can no longer see the frontier separating freedom from slavery. It seems to him there is none.

So?

So: *il veut sa mort*, he wants her/his death.

He thinks this in French, in his own language.

She knows he is thinking in his other language.

A little later, in *Demeure, Athènes*, the panther surprises Jacques Derrida in the middle of the desert. The young soldier thought he had overtaken her, he's walking at a vigorous pace suddenly there she is in front of him, and right away he knows she must have been waiting for him for centuries, crouched down in the shadow of his soul – this sentence is not a simple sentence but who is it? – knowing in advance where to find him – this panther is not only a panther, but who is it? – Who? It's on page 39. "Nous nous devons à la mort." I have it in front of me at this moment, July 19 at noon, printed, timeless, leaning against the clock, disarmed, photographed and enlarged. Even in this mummified state, it still has something frightening about it.

I observe Jacques Derrida in imagination. He has just noted down the message. What a telegram! Telephoned. Nothing is known about the voice. I imagine when God says his speech without words without voice without language without face, he opens his non-eyes he closes his non-eyes, he starts over

Nothing is known about the hour of the expedition either, for God says all the time never long time before and long time after

I observe Jacques Derrida. One can tell from his face that *he can't avoid it*. I have just noted down the words of his expression

Appearing suddenly from one knows not where, like a sentence, like a panther, like the law that puts him in the shade, and the shade is at the same time restricted, closed, no bigger than a grotto, but in its depths it hides endless developments. It will have traversed him without his feeling the pain of it. He flees it and it is in front of him. He becomes its hostage and vice versa, they are tied to each other by an oath that was uttered at their birth, up there in a superior ageless time, a transparent hospitality spreads its tent above them, the sky encircles them. She is large and beautiful dressed in a robe of living gold whose role – in turns sensual poetic and painful – cannot be overemphasized

He caresses her.

She makes him think of – he can't think of it. He caresses, while caressing her whole body from head to tail and all around, a thought. Who are you? Who is it? *Nous-nous-devons-à-la-mort* raises her tail voluptuously, her eyes soften with tears, and when for the third time Jacques Derrida accomplishes pensively this interested caress, she responds by one of those *prr-prr*s come from a throat so deep and powerful that it echoes in the grotto like the last drones of the organ in a church. Understanding now the importance of his caresses he starts over by scratching the flexible vertebrae of the sentence with his fingernails, one after another *nous, nous, de, vons, à, la, mort*. It is like a sensuous song, *nous, nous deux vont à la mort*, we, we two are going toward death. Prr-prr drones the organ. Sometimes he insists on *owe* sometimes on *toward*. Who is death? Whose is it? I am yours, yours, all yours from the throat to the grotto organs the panther. Prrr coos Jacques Derrida. Socrates also coos at the thought of the large woman who is coming toward him, it's in the *Phaedo*.

This cannot last.

"This cannot last" he thinks. "Who is *this?*" she thinks. "It belongs properly to love" he thinks. Sentences succeed one another in his thoughts, he doesn't know if he is pursuing or fleeing them, he doesn't know what they mean to say in truth, he doesn't know if they are fleeing him or if they flee the gaze of the fiancée who sees him thinking but she doesn't know how to read French, she can emit forty-eight love sounds, they are musical versions of *again* and *always*, this he clearly understands.

– This story cannot last, says the lady, how did two people who were so well suited to understand one another end up? says the lady.

It's as if on her side she had met the panther-sentence. A story of two people well suited to understand one another is destined to end says the lady. (Which I regret.)

– Finish, says the lady.

– Why – me? says the gentleman. It's horribly difficult. The thing is done. It is a thing. To say the thing, that's another thing.

All the same he obeys the sentence. After all he is man. He takes his dagger and he finishes it off.

There is carnage. There are panthers with slit throats everywhere.

He seizes a pretext in which he believes. He suspects her based on nothing. He believes she wants to devour him, he thinks of all the women who pass by, of all the voyages he could make if she were not there, thereupon he thrusts his dagger into her neck, "all the same, this is not going to last a lifetime" he says, she rolls while letting out a cry that ices his heart, she thrashes about while looking at him without anger, the desert has never been so horribly beautiful.

The story is finished. We see the gentleman who relates the narrative of the narrator lean over these remains that, posthumously, might be commercialized, for the habit of writing pushes him in that direction, but we see that he comes up against internal difficulties. For him it is indeed finished.

For the killer, who before *that* was the lover and who got mixed up in species and genres, inextricably, to the point of knifing himself in the neck of the panther, not only is it not the end but it is the beginning without end: he can no longer stop loving the object for which he was someone greater and finer than what he has repelled himself into being from then on.

– And Jacques Derrida? Will he have ended by finishing his famous sentence? you say.

– Minute by minute word by word hour by hour, having "the duty to save it" he says, he lends it his body and his ear, that's how he saves life. Up to the last letter.

"I will never forget this sentence" he says, getting on the plane that is taking him back to the other side of the desert, "I leave it without losing it" he thinks (p. 43), in other words without having to kill it to acquit himself of a superhuman promise.

II

THE CAULIFLOWER OF
THE LAUTARET

And you? I say to my mother – what will you never forget?
I will never forget the cauliflower of the Lautaret, says my
mother on July 12, 2003.

The great goddess of Time who governs these centuries
without human measure – we pass by her every day just as she
passes by me ten times a day according to a planetary neces-
sity without paying her any more attention than the sun – is
my mother. She stitches together the events of imperma-
nence, she is whatever assembles and mends the heart's
dislocations. She has lasted for almost one hundred years.
In case of breaks, wounds, suicides of life, losses of blood, she
continues without turning back. Suffering is a kind of bom-
bast that she sobers up. My mother rises behind me and sets
before me, without making any fuss. Eve does not finish.

While I roll my body about on the ground my heart
skewered unable ever to make up my mind to be done with

cares, torments, frights, bitter thoughts, shudders, dreams of burials (of myself or of others) because I fear the cure would make me lose somber pleasures, she is seriously cooking, preparing meals. My castles are thrown into the trash. To be sure among the boxes and crates there is perhaps, hidden, an elevator. The infinite is my limit – I know this in vain. Every one of my mother's sentences is a gold coin, round flat rich. Gives me an extreme pleasure in my mouth. Well, I am utterly incapable of imitating her. I taste with charmed distaste Proust's long sentences drenched in heavy cream sugar honey. I betray myself with rosy-fat-cheeked plump characters even as I cultivate slenderness.

In my interior world, no one is interested in cauliflowers anymore. Ever since my grandmother Omi no longer tells me about Grimm's monstrous cauliflowers, I go so far as to feel contempt for cauliflower.

In a year the two of us have crossed over the Acheron three times, gone through a hundred customs checkpoints, had two passports redone, given recitals in Florida and Tibet with the goal of surviving as usual. I arrive finally, in the train with my mother, on July 13, 2004. The house is only forty-five years old it is much younger than we are and yet it welcomes us with the ancient suppleness of an ancestor. I open BN notebook no. 7 guardian of traces for Montaigne August 2003, New York October 2001 Chicago remains 2002, a little suitcase that smells of past time in the middle of monumental vestiges I find, among the collapsed columns of the world, synagogues and pantheons, the sentence "I will never forget the cauliflower of the Lautaret." It was a year ago.

All at once the sentence happens to me, arrives, on July 13, 2004, suddenly appearing like a young girl in the warm scent of a noon pathway, at the corner of a dream and a waking, everything has already been told-and-forgotten, the sentence now has the charm of the Refound Ones, those unknown faces that one recognizes, those formulas that tickle sleeping memory. I have absolutely no idea who it is, I don't know how old it is, it strikes me as modern, strong, absurd, difficult to interpret, strangely foreign in its French appearance, a touch romantic, gathering round its envelope imprints of hikes and memories of forgetting oneself among mountain peaks, such fatigue and sweat to come a little closer to the sky a cauliflower I say to myself, and in these thoughts where my imagination swings between a great height and the ground floor, I come back to my mother whence the sentence originated a year ago. What is it *the cauliflower of the Lautaret?* I say

Now it's July 14, the firefighters are parading through town. This day is full of echoes of the world's childhood. As one might say the Wolf of the Lautaret. Or the Bear of the Pyrenees. Or the Hydra of Lerna, the Golden Apples of the Hesperides. The place and the character ennoble each other, no one knows who is the lord of the other. The Cauliflower acquires a surplus-value. Then another: it is now the crowning. The summit. The inhabitant. The being has two sexes. Perhaps even the two sexes of the Lautaret. What is a pass? What is the Cauli Flower of a mountain pass?

Finally, I take off. I admit that the idea of cauliflower was weighing down my airplane.

Or else it's the title of a book. One of those promises that hang suspended for a long time above the text. Like *The Charterhouse of Parma*. Or a chambermaid magnified by *In Search of Lost Time*. All the more so because its name is unattractive. Or a pseudonym. It is in any case a password.

– The Cauliflower of the Lautaret? I asked my daughter.

– I have never heard of it. What is it? Is it in a book? Who is it by? If you're thinking of that as a title, it would be a big surprise. Until now you have never talked about vegetables.

– First of all what is the Lotharet? I didn't find it in the dictionary.

– I've heard of the Lot my daughter says. Or else it's the *lot taré*, the spoiled lot?

– The Cauli Flower of the Lot. Now it's turning into a **detective story**.

My daughter and I investigate. – It's the Loch Ness monster, the Beast of the Gévaudan. It's an advertising special for Cauliflower. For literature too. It's delicate. There are always these novelistic conventions. Toponymy is the setting in which characters move around. Finally, I say, it was the Lautaret. This Lautaret makes Cauliflower's fortune. It's like a step up in the world.

I don't even know if you like cauliflower.

– Cauliflower?

You wonder why I am asking you this question. Forty years without cauliflower I say.

– It's not a big deal.

We are not in the same country when I ask you about the cauliflower. That adds a *je-ne-sais-quoi* to the question. An urgency, but undefinable.

Your soft, patient voice, I feel forgiven for all that you do not know, a large indulgence. It's such a mark of trust.

The cauliflower of the Lautaret? says my mother. On her face is spread the face of time.

It's true it was a cauliflower.

Up there we were in snow skiing.

There was an inn

There was a cauliflower gratin

But it was so well done with lots of butter and lots of cheese

That it was really succulent

I'd never eaten anything like it

Such a rich cuisine

We had always eaten low fat. I was when arriving in France

Disgusted that everything was swimming in oil.

– That was when?

– In 1930–31
– But the cauliflower was when?
– The cauliflower was maybe in 32–33
Because we were in the Haute-Savoie.
In the month of March. There was a lot of snow
The Cauliflower of the Lautaret is now seventy-two years
old. Between my mother and the Cauli Flower of the Lautaret
there is the same proximity as between *denken* and *danken*.
My mother is grateful to this Cauli Flower that influenced her
in the French direction despite her reluctance. The Cauli
Flower certainly received the help of contextual powers: one
can imagine mounds of snow in the shape of cauliflower. The
Cauli Flower is itself a mount reduced to a plate. Ever since
the Cauli Flower my mother has remained faithful to the
species.

Today I perfumed myself with lilac water, it's drizzling, I am
at the center, it's an astral day that happens only once every
twenty years or so, in a totally unforeseeable manner. As a
strange attractor, I passed through the same vicinity twenty
years ago, me a blade of straw shaken by random shudders in
the swirling movement of time. One twitches and fidgets. One
feels impossible and gives up. And thereupon, in a totally
random fashion, all the planets that constellate me present
themselves together no one will ever know why. Thus: on July
12 you gave me the invisible ring that you will never have been
able to give me, or to anyone in the world, it is impossible to
predict that this event might ever take place in the lifetime
of those who, having faith, expect nothing, this ring never
existed before, and it is impossible to foresee where it will
reappear in an ulterior manner. This transparent event can be
compared to the sudden appearance of a phrase of a poem,
incredible fate, brief and which in ten years will be engraved

in the dictionaries, retired behind its splendor, quoted in all the cities of the world by those adept in its indecipherable brilliance, never letting the chosen one see more than its back. In truth I cannot say in truth that you gave it to me. I saw its vague shimmering, for that is how it manifests itself. I thought I received and I said nothing.

Thereupon, the telephone rang three times in the morning and from three corners of the world west south and north came the voices of my daughter my son my brother. Each was at liberty in his or her life. A pile of white cows was sleeping near my daughter. My son told the story of the battle waged by talent against genius. My brother had the moving experience of human goodness on the banks of a river.

The proof of God is in coincidences. The pile of cows resembled a large cauliflower in a field.

If childhood memories of mouth and tongue have so much power over our hearts it's because they hold secrets about who we were then. We'd like to press them with questions so they will tell us. We want to go down into the well. The well of the little pies from Carrefour Gaillon that was ten feet deep in 1800 when Stendhal was seventeen years old began to intoxicate him with curiosity when it reached one hundred and ninety feet having added five feet every year. By then he could no longer see the bottom of it. Or the powdered sugar seeping from the young girls in flowers. But a Cauli Flower? It's just like my mother to have chosen for Flower a cabbage I say to myself.

What do you have against cauliflowers? I say to myself

Sometimes one is racist and doesn't know it

With you I live perhaps in a world without cauliflowers?

I am nourished by your words, I can live for months around two words that you have chosen or not, quintessence, play with a verse found again every dawn when coming out of the other world, and which provides me with bread and the place setting of the soul, not forgetting that the soul is made from the finest of the body and when I say months it's a matter of years. But one time I would like to make you a cauliflower gratin, a dish that will have been attained at the end of a long, spiritual and humble climb, a heavenly dish grown on earth, the most ordinary thing there is.

Throughout my mother's whole life, throughout the total of wars and exiles, in Germany, Algeria, France, England, throughout the potato salads throughout voluntary and involuntary journeys and culinary encounters of incalculable number and stories, the Cauli Flower of the Lautaret is a summit in the annals of memory. I have eaten nothing like it, once, an exemplary food that was raised by the devotion of naïveté uniquely characteristic of my mother, to the height of a name. A monument. A book.

I-ate is the visit to a Museum of the living being. I know a person for whom the habit of dining with someone is a staggering blow to the latter's possibility of ever being a legendary character for us. For me, it's the opposite. I have a passionate curiosity to the point of jealousy about what you eat, about what you eat every day, about what we have eaten together, about what we have never eaten together, about what we will one day eat together. Sometimes I ask you on the telephone what you ate for lunch seven hours ahead of and six thousand kilometers away from me and when you give me the precise account of each dish I am in an incestuous state of happiness I swallow your words I feel suckled I think you are my child and all that because of tomatoes with anchovies green beans roast lamb more more and cheese tart to finish. And to think there are books that do not eat.

– So what did you eat? my mother was saying, the urgency with which she interrogated me struck me as nonsense in the past it used to cast a cloud over me, you take my body for my immortal soul I used to say, I bristled, I refused to answer,

I'm not even sure if one evening in Algiers I didn't leave slamming the door, after yelling: you don't love me, I took off, I took the plane. I was fed up with critically annotated menus, you're on the wrong floor I would say to myself, she has always lived on the ground floor or the second floor, my tenth floor doesn't interest her. What's more, it was indiscreet what I eat being only my and your affair from the strictly legal point of view. "What did you read?" she never asked. She wants a confession. I was in revolt, I saw myself as a soul, I would say "my soul." How little one knows oneself. If you had called me my soul, if you said to me "your soul is delicious it's as if when I read your letters I am drinking your soul," I would have been disgusted, I would have felt offended, threatened, I would have headed for the door. When you gave me *Letters from Artaud* to the soul of Genica, what did you want to signify to me? Which one is the vampire? Which of them is not? Is? Drinks the other right on the marrow down to the milk?

With what modern love I prepare my cats' meals, I cook up the meats, mash the vegetables, knead the food with my fingers, I caress their insides, going far beyond the proprieties and ordinary customs I follow with an attentive and gentle finger the most naïve elements of their being, I penetrate into their nature with gratitude, I follow along their life path, their impassioned and constant agitation is the river of my days, they do not cease wanting hoping living questioning savoring watching their machines produce a half-million astonished desires between 6:00 and 9:00 in the morning, they await everything and anything may happen, I study The Cat in medical dictionaries, I hug the cushions, observe the brown spots of their skin, the charming arrangement of beauty spots as if made by india ink on Aletheia's nose, the growth of hair in Philia's ears, each detail is vital, each sign is working, sitting next to you I study the contours of your ear, the folds of the lobes, the attachment of the auricles, the marks of time on the cords of the veins in your neck, the contours of your lines, I take photocopies of your palms and the back of your hands, I have enough for years of geographing you, I feed myself, I don't absorb, I feed, I admire God.

At Olivier de Serres we used to eat English **shortbread** biscuits while drinking Earl Grey tea. These biscuits introduced England into the place called Olivier de Serres. This detail takes its meaning from today. Then I served the biscuits without precisely seeing their importance. I knew very well that they were of my choosing without hesitation that is to say that I vaguely felt a nameless necessity. They were the **shortbreads** that I had gotten into the habit of buying for my long stays in the British Museum. By metonymy the little wedges of pastry had absorbed the voluminous and fertile idea of the most substantial library in the world. To eat **shortbreads** was to let melt on your tongue the sacred host of venerated books. I read you. *Hoc est meum corpus* and your body was also for me the bread of all the venerated books. I felt and didn't know how to read in the time in the desert, I was choosing, so I believed, in truth I was obeying messages dictated by the divine urgency of life, it was my life that chose for me. I could no longer not buy **shortbreads** in their boxes decorated with Scottish motifs. According to my mother the least expensive are at Marks & Spencer. This is her way of venerating life, the cult of thriftiness. And to think it took me thirty years to get beyond the deafness that stretched between my mother and me. I didn't understand her language and I didn't know it. I was hopelessly bad at translation, I didn't even think about it, given my obscurantist conviction at the time, like someone without faith who doesn't know there is faith, that we were all living in French, while in fact we were living on fragments of continents cut off from blood since prehistory, I annexed her to my own tendencies, coming from her I thought, she comes down to me, she was part of my furniture, but poorly maintained by her, I had ingested her and I would get angry that she dared to inquire about my digestion.

It's only yesterday that I began to meet her outside of my book, to leaf through her like a book that I had never bothered to open, to observe her like a tribe about which I am astonished and pleased to know strictly nothing and from which I have everything to learn so as finally to measure against her singularities my own oddities of which I'm unaware. Today when Eve asks me: "What did you eat?" with that serious hope that makes her eyes sparkle, I say: "And you?" That's what she's waiting for. She tells me everything, shows a merciless severity for non-successes, tolerates with rapidity and exactness human foolishness, gets carried away with a harsh naïveté into moral philosophy instead of staying in the kitchen which alone is her subject; but it's difficult not to be led there, because the kitchen, as a room for testing virtues, is the center of all truths. "To doubt is to waste; instead I taste" says my mother. Eve often goes to restaurants. It's not a matter of accumulating but of thinking: how is it done? What is a dish? And the language of the dish? Might there be (but one) ethics and politics of cooking that is not irresponsible and yet carried by imagination?

– What interests me is what the Great Cook does, says my mother. I have always loved the Great Cooks. Hake on top of the filets he puts basil leaves, peppers, tapenade. I get ideas that I don't try out. What interests me: the art. I note everything, and I don't redo it. I watch these great artists. It's a pleasure. Not to eat it. From the health point of view I'm against it. There were also shellfish in the picture. The Great Cook is an artist. Of living. You see that it's beautiful and it's good. This cooking is not made to be eaten. It's a question of changing all these fish into painting. I watch the Great Cook, I travel in extraordinary countries that stomachs dream of. The Great Art that tastes only with the eyes and ears. It's good and it's beautiful a recounting of the dream of food.

Eve does not remember ever having had a good meal in a restaurant. Once with Fred thirty years ago on my directions. But she remembers all those bad meals. Restaurants are inter-estaurants, says my mother. She savors her invention by laughing so hard she cries.

– What did you do with Olivier de Serres? you say.

Today June 5, 2004, is the first time we admit between us that something besides us may have happened at Olivier de Serres.

Olivier de Serres is neither past nor present. For a long time I was against the idea of selling the secret. Then I let be sold the outer shell of the Nest. One can't return in reality to the dream of Olivier de Serres. The nest is no longer. The walls remain. They have put a cement step in the middle of the wooden stairs says my mother.

In reality it was awful but you liked it says my mother because it was an old building altogether antique. I don't know if you ever lived there. It was calm and near a market district that you never took advantage of.

I went there as I go to dreams, entering my bed in the evening the way one slips into the ghost ship, knowing neither where the night will cast me, onto which shore, upon which island or into which gulf or district, nor whether I am going to draw life or death.

When you go to Olivier de Serres you always find yourself awaited by me at all times.

– You're the one who bought it, says my mother. I don't want to know about it. I have forgotten. I can't remember. To have bought, sealed, I can't. When I make these nesting gestures, I don't tell anyone, I forget.

These places are too dangerous, these landing strips that it's a matter of turning into huts.

Will you land on Monday? Let's hope.
Where to find it again? When? In bed. Come. Turn out the
light. Wait. If it's not in this dream, maybe in the next one.

Olivier de Serres, you say. We say: "Olivier de Serres" and
we find ourselves again in the tiny dark room, hanging hug-
ging, it's right before the story, the way we crawled toward one
another, into one another, urged on by terrorized natural laws,
the Thing-that-wants before the name before all the names
Olivier de Serres, primary nest. "Olivier de Serres": the key.
Never thought, always said – the true words, the keywords.
Two big cats, but without fur, instead of the magnificent
armored coats with which the Great Cook has dressed the
panthers, delight of the painters, we are enveloped hidden in
the over-unders of the sixties, corseted dressed up sheltered in
an entanglement, but destined to be hastily torn off sometimes
with those four hands mixed with paws, claws withdrawn.
It smells of dust. Primal grotto. Musty nest, dens, uneasy
appetite, obligatory – the frightening strictness of – of what –
of the "senses," the word sense, we used to say this word:
sense. You sense my senses? Those things in the body
that sniff, grumble, grunt, want, immorally extramortally
extramorally *Want*. Who can resist this weakness of Wanting,
these animals in the body that leap, attack, have the invincible
strength of hunger's fire, know nothing of no, know nothing
of noun, only the verb: eat, *manger*, *man-ger*, grab, *man-
ger*, the magic word *m'anger*, angel me. Mama's word: eat!
Promise. Mmm. Mamamam, I have mm mmeaten.
We ate one another. We gnawed one another out of raging
hunger for *mamanmanger*, so we threw ourselves on the lamb
that mama had slaughtered for us to eat and brought back
delicately in her jaws to Olivier de Serres, agronomist. He is
the author of *Le théâtre de l'agriculture et mesnage des champs*,

The Theater of Agriculture and the Tending of the Fields (1600).

Still blind and sticky we sucked the heavy Olivier de Serres milk. He introduced into France mulberries, hops, madder and mulberries. Several times we say mulberries, madder. The marriage of mulberry and madder. The marriage of the Olivier and the Serre, the Olive Tree and the Greenhouse. One can't escape the hidden designs of God. *She* has written everything down *and* we do not read. We are read. Without Olivier no mulberry no worm no silk no female pine cones and cannabinaceae no female intoxication no military red.

"All the same, this is not going to last a lifetime," that is one of the thoughts that crawls through the humid Olivier de Serres darkness, "that would be unlivable" we think, "it's too much" you say, "enough! no more," eating each other again so darkly so raw, pinching each other red this clash of unknown animals in which we are dissolved boiled resuscitated, this untamable *mesnagerie* in which we enclose ourselves once we cross the filthy threshold of Olivier de Serres, this cannot last.

We never think Olivier. We enter and we fall. We fall into the sticky breast of the eagle. Its *serres*, that is, its talons are inside obviously. As they are God's talons they are immense we are in the gentle grip of his paws, we don't think, it's to be undergone. It's not our fault. It's stronger than we are, God Olivier de Serres, we are in the darkness of the breast in no name. Between cats between rages between panthers between bodies: no name. The name is the error. I mean: it is the exterior. The exterror. The destruction of the burrow.

The sorrows of the French soldier's soul heated to alizarin red by the desert, in other words by the purity of the passion, are all caused by the error of a name. At the beginning of this story was: the beginning. The necessary desert and no one. The nameless being, formerly a soldier, alone. The being with the brightly colored coat and of the female sex who pants non-humanly, who is comparable to a rose and pink like a rose in her grotto is likewise nameless. I say. She is much larger than he. Little by little he lets himself be conquered by the beautiful one, he moves away from his kind, he rolls around in the secret of the fabric of the rich fur, he takes the tuft that tops her formidable tail and puts it in his mouth, he's like a young dog playing with his master letting himself be rolled about beaten flattered, he surprises her by growling under his tongue. They make love. Then he makes the error: (1) he speaks French to her (2) he gives her a name (3) the name is shabby. This is the first step toward nothingness. Under the blow of the name she is already no more than a shriveled husk.

As long as she's alive he doesn't know how much he loves her. He becomes a character in a novel. The novel follows its course. There are no more surprises. He loses the desert. A long time later on a foreign battlefield he loses the leg that she had nibbled and for which he had murdered her. He doesn't pay much attention to this. After all it's merely a cadaver's leg. All his great torments died with his panther. Words as well remained behind in the sands. The misfortune is that now he drags this cadaver around in a horrible absence of desert. Between us never any name. Except Olivier de Serres. Still today June 2004 no name blows. Between Antonin Artaud and Genica Athanasiou, no name, only dear dear dear lovely lamb sweet woman always angel, X, but Come my sweet woman, dear dear dear until the day when – it's around the end of June 1923 he thinks she wants to devour him not knowing the pain he has caused her and without waiting he is the first to strike he plunges a Genica in her neck, and it's over. Each time he says Genica to her it's a letter telling her: I will not see you tomorrow the more gentle docile patient I make myself the more I reduce myself restrain myself the more you hollow me out, you dig your claws into me in those parts of me located behind my consciousness and that I cannot reach, you penetrate me with your muscular tail topped by black rings, you have stripped me of my Provençal Frenchman's skin right down to the buttons and the buttonholes, you shake me up your panting spirit terrifies my past, I'm beginning to think I should have left with your voice, closed myself up in Solitude with an elective emotion in harmony with your voice that I learned how to imitate, you are a witness, lover of my person instead of letting myself be transformed into an ultimaton and ultimatman by a woman who did so while not being up to the level of my genius, Genica, completely the opposite.

It is horribly difficult to send one another/oneself and receive letters that are so threatening for the spirit's soul, the heart's soul, the life's soul, the soul of things, in the absence of soul without the body's letter for all letters are photos of howls of fright. Still today I wonder why you sent them to me. Was it in order to say to me: "It is not I who write you these letters. It is you"?

Yesterday, I passed in front of Olivier de Serres you say. The taking of Olivier de Serres is the flip side of contemporary history, I say. It's one of the countless oddities resulting from the Algerian wars. I'm wearing a long coat embroidered with bloody thorns, when I arrive in Paris I get entangled in the folds of savage memories, there are carpets even in the stairways of the buildings to smother the cries, what was I in this Salon? Disgusted, the more I walked around Paris, the more I was thrown off track, I was headed toward failure, this kingdom is waging a perfidious and ancient war against me which I don't know how to play. No one said anything to me, but I was forewarned of ambushes, persecution cannot go any further. I'll give an example: the Luxembourg garden. I tried five or six times to cross it without success, whichever direction I took. I enter. To have pruned trees on a piece of ground, I see in that a denunciation of my whole being. I ignore it, I advance, some undergrowth comes along, I could tame my disheveled body with so many scenes that depict my incongruity, those slow-walking actors those children playing ball, at each step one might think one was at the master's door, but thereupon all the same some undergrowth comes along, I would not be surprised, but I'm dreaming, to see a broom flower rise up so I am saved. Upon which, exactly the opposite: above all you must not stay here, that's what is launched in my direction by a fleeing passer-by whom I don't have the time to see, move away, quick hide in the grass, under the bridge, for what you see coming from over there, which you above all should not see, you must above all not let them discover you, it's the army of the Salon, there already entering the narrow path secretly cut through the bushes, the first uniforms with their vehicles, thrones, tribunals and dominations and behind them the whole army is going to arrive, that army of the entitled and know-how that will kill anyone who makes trouble. I had just enough time to slip to the side. I never managed (to arrive at) the Luxembourg. In New York I used to walk along the heights, even on foot in Central Park I was in the heights. The first poem also, the one that began by *Never*, in the heights.

In Paris I found myself all the time in the subway, brought down, a reject, I went to the extreme of banishment. How to find you again? I spent my days running around everywhere.

I had my mother buy Olivier de Serres unseen. I walked by it, in a foreign land in Paris a North African't, a *maugrébine* among the French she in Algiers a midwife Rue d'Isly me at twenty lost among the corners of French boulevards, I am guided by the passion that doesn't know where it is, I get into a deserted subway car where I spread out my books, my files, I'm seated on the floor my young cat jumps up on the empty benches, suddenly the train moves off, I should get out, but

I don't have the strength to gather up my dispersion, I am obsessed by love, lost in my papers, how can I arrive somewhere in the everyday, whereupon I find myself dumped, with my cat in my arms, in front of the entrance to an old dwelling for sale, necessity advises me not to hesitate. Everything that happens is imperious. I paid with lemons from Algiers. Real lemons, wild, scented, pure, that I have never found again since in any country, fat and yellow, adorable in their goodness and consolation, each one wrapped like a big-bellied king in a piece of newspaper, the *Alger républicain*, putting my hands on these bellies saved me from the madness of exile. I owe a survival to the golden lemons of Algiers.

– Since you couldn't send money from Algeria says my mother, I generally found some tricks in a box of clothes or food for my daughter. When I arrived at the port where one turned over packages to customs the guy who was circling round them I used to give him some change and it would get through. One day I arrive the guy says to me you have to go through the police, obviously I had a good sense of smell, a sixth sense, says my mother. That day I had put gold pieces at the bottom of the box I put a false bottom on top then I put lemons from the garden each lemon wrapped in a newspaper. When he got to the third lemon the guy was fed up and the package passed. The worst was when it arrived at your place. You can't talk in letters. I sent you the lemons counting on your sense of smell I tell you.

And it's true that I was carried away by the scent.

Some time later when I arrive at my daughter's here for Olivier de Serres, says my mother, did you get my package?

– With the lemons? I say.

– The lemons! says my mother. There was gold under the false bottom and you saw nothing?

– The box, I said, I threw it away

– A box full of gold! In appearances my daughter trusts! Hélène always throws away all the principal.

So all the same we looked in the basement, in the storage rooms. In the furnace room. And *what did we see? The box.* The keeper of the building had kept the box because it might be useful.

– How was I to know?

– Know! You have to have a sense of smell. I couldn't put the dots on all the i's. Because of this scare, I paid for Olivier de Serres without looking, says my mother. Once bitten twice shy. That place was awful, you liked it.

There was no view, Olivier de Serres was a ground-floor lair. That detail must have pleased me, today it would horrify me. Once inside, we were no longer anywhere, I found hope again that left me as soon as I entered the exterior world.

In Paris among the French I was dying of follies, as I've already said, I ate dates, I sometimes looked at the dingy city squares my teeth chattered.

It's as if I had bought a bed of dreams with the golden lemons.

As soon as one entered, it was life at the highest pitch, a step and one was sailing down one's own veins everything simple that happened was like the last hour before death. Two hours of Olivier de Serres and one emerged in tears, the heart tired of redreamliving. Every minute had its double, as if it were counted, as if this recess were a résumé of subterranean descents with climbs back up. The diffuse impression that I make out very long afterwards: never were we, had we been, would we be as alone as unknown thus as improbable as buried without address as ephemeral; and yet there was someone, this is something I manage to grasp only today, there was besides the two of us, apart from you and apart from me, another part, a presence, something that preceded us, that followed us, it was not the place, it resided in the place, something like a thought but located above and beyond us, something like an author but who didn't intervene, who would merely remember, with what difficulty I evoke today this capital and uncertain detail, I am perhaps deluded

this presence – I feel it – was not of the present but something like an observation, a cominglater, like someone who would say to himself, to herself: we'll see.

It seems to me that we felt ourselves seen. Not under surveillance, but bet on. In dispute. It seems to me that we were very small, awkward, we mistook the word timidity for the word temerity and vice versa. And ready to flee. For example I never entered the obscure Olivier de Serres without casting about a circular glance, not to see someone, but out of astonishment, and so as to penetrate there soul first.

It's that no one ever saw us enter or leave. There is no proof.

Today we call all that: god. These passings, these overflights of birds, these unfolding absences, these varieties of fear, these crossings between species: god.

It was a young Tuesday, I knew right away it was ours, all the anguish of the Salon had just disappeared like phantoms at the break of day, and the day had broken – like the instant we found ourselves again in that absurd place. It was an airy hour, I was filled with a joy-of-Juliet, that pure joy which after her death she left at the disposal of couples who refind one another on the other side of separation, a joy that transforms everything into joy, even jealousy becomes joylousy. If you felt like hanging yourself, this joy would unhang you. Oh – to climb toward you, despite the smell of grease in the alleyway, to feel the sky even in the wall cracks a creeping ivy changed into wings, to find you again, clear the obstacles and each obstacle is an added felicity. Finally you're there, the heights are caught in the curtains, you arrive in the little room that is my other body, you enter, it's you it's me organs salted in sweat, violent heartbeats, my whole being beats in you or else

toward you, there is no more world except time and time is
not made of time, it's a fire on which to suck, eyes rolled back
into mouths that moan with delight and also because there are
no words in this place made divine. You are quick hurried
slightly teasing. You say to me: you know I have come from
the play across the way. They were showing a film, they had
staged a rehearsal. A Shakespeare comedy. I was obliged to
make love with that woman for pedagogical reasons. – Which
comedy? – You're not bothered that I have come directly from
there? – From the rehearsal?

But I love you so much. I want you so much, the door
behind you where things have happened is closed, the
rehearsal of the comedy is closed on its secret, there is no
knowing in Olivier de Serres, only happiness in everything, in
the parts and in the degrees. I burst out laughing, my desire is
powerful, I will carry you off you'll see and then we are at one
another caresses rock us we mistake egos and it's a single silky
self that we spread over our body, I faint from sweetness on its
breasts, I take it up again one by one, true, a joking little rage
comes to my lips: has he been touched here? on the chest? on
the nape? the panther growls softly, "So help me God, I think
she is jealous" says the character in the comedy, but the power
of love is stronger than all, the silk marries its subtle tints with
the tanned shades that distinguish his thighs from my thighs,
all this time has a soul, we think, golden like us, unique,
solitary, and burning, like us, we feel. Olivier de Serres in that
instant of wonderment gushes fountains on a garden of virgin
thickets of French gardeners and these diffuse images are the
exact concrete expression of Tuesday's trembling youth, the
world forgotten. At noon the dream begins to enter me and it
is absolute nourishment. Eat, *mangez*, angels, angels. At that
moment – Interruption. The two cats scurry away. Someone
comes in. We break off. Me who wants to be born. It's one of
the neighbors. Surely we are going to get rid of him quickly,

not let him come between us. Me who wants to drink with you at the birthplace of water. But to my great fury you detain the young man who is getting ready to leave, you say: have you seen this reproduction? You are obeying the laws of hospitality. You are polite. I am trying to die to the world, but the young man leaps at the chance, he takes hold of this copy of a modernist painting, he begins to praise it. Is there a happiness on earth? Olivier de Serres is betrayed and Paris is everywhere. I am pierced through with pain. Did I not already have to overcome the traces of the comedy? And now it's the desert that is trampled underfoot. Anger grabs me. A monkey escapes upstairs and I recognize myself in his feverish flight. In an instant I tumble down from the balcony. What heights we had reached without effort! I slide all the way down. Sands, sands, erase them. Once Below, pain and impatience flood my heart. One cannot flee these fires. And you didn't look for me. And you didn't bend down to sound the abyss. And I tread alone the infinite sands. I miss you. Monkey, monkey, here I go coming back up, I want to find you again, I want to have you. In a few instants I'm on the third landing, I raise my head I don't see you on the fourth level but doubtless you're in some corner of the fifth degree, I climb up to the skin of the sky. The circular stage is empty. You are not there, you have left. True, it was I who left, but it's you who was left to me. Oh horror of the void, dread of the desert, where have you hidden yourself? But it occurs to me that you have gone back to France. The complete absence of any sign turns me into a three-year-old child ripe enough to feel pain and crazy from impotence. I lose my memory. I remember only one detail of this hour of agony. It's a sheet of paper. "Call me" you wrote. It's you, it's your writing, and you thought to add your telephone number which I know by heart. Thus you know I have lost my head. But Olivier de Serres has no telephone. Here I go taking off again like a woman mad with pain, running around to everyone, knocking on shutters, on doors, "We haven't seen him" that's the title of this sequence, endured so many times, how long will this Tuesday last, how will this dream end?

Although we were not able then to imagine its future developments, the Telephone motif began with Olivier de Serres, the divinity of the implacable, the most tenacious of our demons.

Again yesterday, a cherished day when you had just returned from a trip. I have only one means of distracting my impatience finally to hear you – it is to busy myself with social semblances, I make vague approaches to serious colloquia, I listen to ten orators as if they were but one, a single speech interests me, and I'm awaiting its hour, I feel as if I'm translating *The Aeneid* approaching in slow movements the moment when the absent ones come back, among whom myself who is hidden far from my body in your thought. Refreshments are served. I act exactly as if I were there. Now I am approaching the Hour. In two minutes you will enter your office. Your telephone will ring. It will be my voice. At this moment I'm struggling to turn on my mobile. This little jewel is recalcitrant. In vain I key in the formula, it remains unmoved. You imagine my anxiety. A few friendly people are observing me. One faded lady of grayish appearance proposes to give me a hand: she specializes in these little objects. In my confusion, I entrust the little one to her. And I dare ask Lucifer for permission to make a brief call on her own mobile. That way I will tell you in a few brief coded words what the matter is and as soon as my mobile is cured I will call you. Suddenly the moment I dial your number a voice in me says: madness! This alien mobile will keep the trace of the secret. And I stop myself. At that instant I'm seized by a premonition. Where is the grayish lady? I *know* in a flash that she's gone off with her loot. It was a theft. The idea had grazed me, and was repulsed right away. I am so touchy as soon as it's a question of telephones. And still not enough. Yet it's a matter of life and death. Now here I am voiceless. So close to you. And like someone with a slit throat. No later than yesterday.

And the telephone with the cardboard keys, last summer you remember? How have two people so well suited to understand one another managed to survive?

In most stories two people suited to understand one another end up killing one another. They say: there is a misunderstanding. They act as if there was a misunderstanding. From passion one passes into fiction. There was always misunderstanding.

It was during the long hours when hope abandoned him that he amused himself with the panther. He had thus already abandoned the panther. He betrayed, distracted himself with her, he betrayed her, all the evil was waiting to leap on her. He didn't want to be the first to kill her first. Who will have begun? On one side and the other.

Each time I go to the Maison de la Radio I pass by Olivier de Serres, by the nest of the first time I say, I don't stop, I have never thought to stop, if I stopped, if I approached, the former nest would become a tomb, a monument, I pass by, in front of, I think in front of, I remember the first chapter of the book that I have not reread, that I will never reread, fortunately Olivier de Serres is not in the front, I never see its face, Olivier de Serres is dug out in the back of the Rue de la Convention, if Olivier de Serres had disappeared we wouldn't know it, but I believe Olivier de Serres is still in its crevice, Olivier de Serres lives on in the descendants of the golden lemons of Algiers, he is a contemporary of Montaigne, on June 5, 1562, he goes to Rouen where Montaigne also goes following the king's army, during the religious troubles. What interests them, each from his side, is to meet the indigenous Brazilians who are passing through this still Huguenot city. There is talk of unknown essences. People try to speak a little this other language. Back home in Montaigne the lord has mulberry trees planted in the courtyard of the château.

But we don't know anything about it.

And yet.

A story doesn't begin at the beginning. Later it starts to have begun a long time ago no one knows how. Time, that doesn't mean anything. I say: "forty years ago," forty doesn't mean anything. The time is the same time. I say: forty. Forty says to me: "Forty years in the desert." Forty years in the desert is a long time. Forty years in passion is yesterday. 'Forty years that went by just like that, *comme ça*' you say.

At that moment the word *ça* grabs hold of my mind with an incredible force for such a little vocable. *Ça*: it, that, this, indefinite, nameless

At that moment I hear an extremely loud and strange minuscule chirping. Just the way a human being's howl of pain must sound to a god passing by far away: minuscule very loud, smaller than a cricket's howl but as strident. It ululates. Like a faraway god I hear cricketing clicking the it, the *ça*, terrorized by the smallness that we are. We are so small and the great-ness is so great. We are the little insect of life and the Great Threat lies in wait for us. Heard from extremely high. What is striking is the enormous force of weakness.

The being who cries is human.

I am sitting next to you on the divan and suddenly it cries, there are cries from a corner behind the door, a minuscule cry able to rise from the depths of a forty-year well. I see nothing. It is not an insect. It's a being.

Now I see the two cats frozen in front of it. Finally I see *it*, you see that? The being who cries: I'm alive, alive, alive, alive!

is a tiny field mouse. Suddenly my cats are giants, they are mountains who pace back and forth with slow rapidity.

How small *It* is, it's exactly the size of life defending itself in the face of condemnation. The dwarf that we are with a voice that overcomes time. I who am It, you and we I who am the cats and the seven dwarves of anguish, I must.

I am seated by your side, then you say: "Forty years that went by just like that." More dead than alive: and yet saved. The mouse is no longer here or there. Between the terrible portions he escaped.

I will never forget that cry I say.

I understood the mouse. It was not a complaint. It was an indignant affirmation. "One has no right to kill me as long as I'm alive," "Alive, alive, alive!" Finally I no longer see the mouse I no longer hear him. He must have given death the slip.

"Good, smile!"[2] you say to me.

If, God forbid, I found the body, I would not tell you. There are things one must not say.

How does *Ça* happen? Where does *Ça* live? Where does *Ça* hide. *Ça* does not want to die. *Ça* is an indefinite pronoun. You don't know what you're talking about when you say *ça*. *Ça* is not *ci*? *Ça* leaves. That doesn't mean *ça* doesn't come back.

Olivier de Serres is a primary school, a native city, we return to it in thought, we pass by, we beg it to keep our memories until after our death.

I am accompanied by words. Preceded followed by powerful words. Watched over by supernatural words.

Every time I go to certain places, theaters, castles, train stations, hotels, lecture halls, hospitals, a word falls upon me

---

[2] That is, "Bon, souris!" *Souris*, the second-person familiar imperative of *sourire*, to smile, is a precise homonym of *souris*, mouse. So he also says "Good, mouse!" (Tr)

These words, these *mots*, are not only words of language.
They are motors.

Little words, for example? No. You never sent me what in
French we call *un petit mot*, "a little word," as Albertine does
to the narrator and vice versa. Between us no "little words."
Brief, sharp, strong words.

Word-things, word-plants. Passwords remarkable for their
insignificance. These *ças* are like marvelous little thumps on
the violin partition that the grandmother and the child narra-
tor play, that messenger partition of the morning capable of
rendering all the nuances of feeling, the invisible partition
susceptible to thought's least flutter that speaks between
Eurydice and Orpheus, saying so exactly I desire above all to
ask you what I desire above all not to ask you for fear of waking
you if you are sleeping, disturbing you if you are busy, retain-
ing you if you are in a hurry, do you hear me? I don't dare
knock more than once very lightly, don't wake up, please wake
up – I want you to come I don't want to ask you to come I am
asking nothing of you, don't listen to that slight little noise on
the violin partition, don't hear it, I merely want to know if you
are there, do you exist, don't answer me, are you walking right
beside me, does heaven exist, I ask nothing more of God than
a very slight little tap, coming to answer yes to my question,
did I even hear it, I ask nothing more of God than the taps
meant to say to the child, it's his translation from the grand-
mother's side: "Don't worry yourself, little mouse, I am going
to come," these maternal Morse taps, I ask God for them, for
above all I fear obliging you to come.

I am not making anything up. On my left I have *Sodom and
Gomorrah* leaning, both of them, lightly, on the telephone
from which I eternally await the maternal taps that fend off
death. I am dead but I'm holding on. I want to wake up but it
cannot be up to me. You alone, grandmother, can come to the
aid of my being, you alone know why and how living is a cat

and mouse fight, and that cats are a kind of giant mice, there is no other danger than the pains and sorrows mice inflict on themselves. Why, otherwise, does the grandmother answer the supplicant by calling him "little mouse"? When I knock on the violin partition, I am outside of life, and you inside. All that's needed is for your telephone to ring that is to say the telephone-your-messenger and the partition dissolves. I call you grandmother that is to say life. My mother as well, it sometimes happens that she is my grandmother. This occurs when she is shuttling between death and life "Don't worry yourself, little mouse, I understand you're impatient, but I am going to come."

Of the two of us you're the one who comes back most often. I found the most beautiful sentence imaginable in words of the world in one of the volumes of the *In Search of Lost Time*, not very long ago. I don't know how I failed to notice it earlier. And one thinks one is reading.

This sentence has become for me the ideal of happiness in writing. It is a sentence from the two sides in other words from the two languages, that of the heart and that of dream, that of sadness and that of jubilation. It says, then, on p. 762 in this edition:

"*Tu sais bien pourtant que je vivrai toujours près d'elle, cerfs, cerfs, Francis Jammes, fourchette.*"[3]

No sooner said than it begins to disappear like a mouse, and yet it is imperishable. It is the most unique, the mad one,

---

[3] These words are the last spoken by Proust's narrator in one of his dreams about his grandmother after her death. They may be roughly translated as: "You know I will always live close to her, deer, deer, Francis Jammes, fork." Upon awakening, the narrator professes to have lost all insight into the sense of the word sequence: "the sequence of these words had ceased offering me the limpid and logical sense that they expressed so naturally for me just a moment before and that I could no longer remember." The French word *cerfs* is an exact homonym of *serres*, as in Olivier de Serres. (Tr)

the poem. All alone she would probably be closed up in an asylum. But it is surrounded by millions of sentences that protect it and give it the strength to be delirious in peace. It is the queen bee. The entire book deploys its industry so she can spread her insane wings. And thereupon, without any natural escort, without circumspection, a small fire breaks out, without any mad rolling of the eyes, without seeking to produce an effect, almost as monstrously innocent as my mother coming almost naked or without almost out of her *donche* to tell me dripping wet while hanging on the door of the bathroom the memory, which just made her burst out laughing eighty years after the event, of Kurt Jonas, a genius, but who, up until his premature death, took the letter *u* to be the letter *n*, and thus a *donche* instead of a *douche*, a shower. Nymph, nymph, *donche*, *fourchette*. *Fourchette* is genius. The signature of Life. *Cerfs*, *cerfs* is the spirit of Olivier de Serres, an oath of Life sworn on the head of the grandmother.

This is a sentence from the camp of life. Such lively animation around the grandmother's bed. How could she stay dead?

Fourchette is the name of my next cat.

Olivier de Serres, I thought while passing in my car five meters from the entrance to the grotto, and this causes a very slight itch in my left shoulder. Trace of a claw mark. What else.

– I don't remember the layout of the place, you say.

– One enters through the minimal corner kitchen and right away on the right is the little one-person bed, the curtains are always drawn, the only thing we do here is make love, but what does that mean make love? if one could make what no one in the world can make? all the same that's the expression we favor because it is distractingly mad

One cannot live in this grotto, only fall tremble, fear, despair in secret, wait. There is no telephone. Only miracles. Waiting.

There must be a non-bedroom to begin the Desert. A cell always.

– The place had no layout, I say. We fell holding one another tight onto the narrowness of the divan.

It is places that make love. Places and all their features. For them to make love (and so that they might do so), the features must combine their forms, their different energies and their properties in a whole whose total makes god. Each element retains a power. Passionate beings that find refuge in the Place have not the least idea of the minute qualities of this place. That there is no telephone is a rational inconvenience commanded by the distressed respect that I owed it to myself to show my mother to whom I owe everything, after the affair of the golden lemons. She keeps a close eye on my bills. – A telephone for whom? – No telephone.

A telephone for *cerfs, cerfs*.

We have no number, no line. An English chest of drawers for nothing.

Without the absence of telephone none of the encounters whose consequences are still presently incalculable could have taken place. By going around my mother's innocence, I could have had the telephone installed?

One could not think of *installing* anything. The idea of a refrigerator, no. If not the thing, at least the idea but there was perhaps a decrepit one, since there was a water heater? Each desert was crossed hopefully, with a hope crouching in ambush. To hope also takes a toll. I hid my hoping, I went so far as to hide hope from myself. To ask for more than one chance, a splendid survival, doesn't befit Olivier de Serres. One moves on to the stars. I live the book of chances, my heart twice gnawed at by anxieties which were to be withstood with a military docility. All these thoughts remain in the spectral state, they do not crystallize. One has be content with god, without the proper word. But all the almost-words are put forward, used, without understanding. We speak to one another like cats. Suddenly I make an urgent speech to you, uttered in a pressing voice, and you know that I have *said something* to you it was important, that you know that I said to you. You know.

I never said to you: come back.

Each time that you left forever, I lowered my head I looked at your left hand, I looked at the white carpet in front of the divan on which we were sitting, I didn't say the word, there is no circumstance, then I raised my eyes and looked out the window at the world that was moving away with the solemn slow pace of an ocean liner, it looked like an entire country was setting out to sea with its towers on the right, on the left its cathedrals, in the middle its hospital roofs, an airplane was showing off across the sky, and was heading for foreign lands. How did I keep from killing myself? There was the law of freedom that I couldn't infringe without killing. I whispered to myself the ending prayer: "You know well however that I will always live close to your life *cerfs cerfs* Olivier de Serres, *fourchette*." You had already crossed the river, whereupon the sequence of magic words very quickly lost its limpidity and in the instant I no longer remembered. I barely said to myself: "for how long will you remain gone forever?" and the logic of these words that expressed themselves before me without any possible doubt had escaped me. You came back each time you naturally came back it was naturally that time there, the unique one, absolutely unexpected, I was the first one to be astounded by it, I no longer even understood the absence, I woke up, I looked out the window, the divan sat facing the world, I no longer even understood how I had been able to live so long in the desert without passion, some dreams lasted for years, two or three but I was suffering them for twelve or twenty, I thought I was dying. I thought: dying, is that all it is, *n'est-ce que ça?* This imbecility, this suppression of myself against which I was voiceless and worldless and no one to whom to say "I was, in the past" "I knew the King well" still less.

III

THE FIRST LUCIDITY

On July 8, 2004, I abruptly put my writing office in order. I don't know why. This consists of ejecting the occupants of the top three shelves, hundreds of books that have been lying there for forty years. Abruptly today, it's their last day. I arrived in the house a half hour ago. I stand on a chair. I plunge my arms into the dust. It's a revolt. I obey. Who? Dozens of art books, novels, I don't know what all. Among these dumped piles sleeping in Hell I find files of notes taken while I was preparing my thesis on Joyce. The situation is reversed: I see myself obliged to look carefully at what I was going to throw out. If only I could see J. J. my teacher in 2004 once more!

Instantly I am like Henry Brulard hoping in 1836 to see once more Mme Le Brun now the Marquise de G. who was surprised at H. B.'s total silence in 1800 to ply her with questions – so that she might tell him *who* he was then, so that he might tell me who I was when I felt that no one understood me. She was a witty woman she must be close to seventy years old today. I kept silent in Paris instinctively I spoke only with my thesis director, a Jansenist, another Pascal, a man of ferocious integrity, J. J. But it's impossible. I see J. J. only in dreams and when we meet during one of his visits to the living he has many other important things to tell me.

I scan these vestiges of the prehistory of the pupil I was, I don't recognize myself. All of this is very scholarly, proper, and not straying from the road so as to follow the cliff that wavers on its pedestal. There's no foam, no trembling. It doesn't induce fright, not even shame. There is nothing wrong. I could deposit these drafts at the BN without fearing some future righteous malevolence. There is also a card from the **Reading Room** of the British Museum. It's indeed a question of me. I was thus in my mental underground on 1.9.1963, **Letter and no. of Seat L II**, I had requested the work *James Joyce: Two Decades of Criticism.* The latter was: **in use** by a Mr Penman. **If urgently required apply to Superintendent** This sign of presence at a distance takes on an incredible importance today. I see myself seated beneath the lamp in September 1963, my problem, my companion, and my sniggerer is Joyce, now there's a man and a dead man whose opinion I do not fear. Right after that I get lost in New York. You fall upon me.

In another scholarly folder I find a letter from my thesis director J. J. It was sent from the University of Paris in 1965, it arrives at destination in 2004. It is addressed to the one I was then in the one I then am. It is a certificate of delirium. The master says: "At the end of two delirious years, when there were traces of delirium in your writing, you have now reached a second lucidity, more fertile than the first, *stronger.*" He underlines *stronger.* Twice and in close proximity, he uses the words delirious, delirium, which is not recommended. He underlines only *stronger.*

I recognize lovingly his beautiful, regular, and well-formed handwriting, his delicately worked *d*s descended from Greek

deltas, the cadenced harmony of his paragraphs, "yes" he says
– it's about my reflections on Joyce, then "yes, yes," "that's it."

I feel a happiness of relief. "I certify," says the master, "that
the researcher H. C. was delirious for two years at the end of
which she reached a second lucidity." Yes and *yes*. The first and
the second.

I met you in the middle of my first lucidity.

I'm not exactly sure if I was in the first or the second lucid-
ity when I bought Olivier de Serres so as not to live there.

I'm extraordinarily relieved to have found this certificate of
disarray arrayed or disarrayed in these volumes of papers con-
cerned with Joyce's *Ulysses*. I don't remember having received
this letter or in what state of mind. Today it arrives like a test
result. It shows that I was not delirious during my long delir-
ium. I was in a half-light of lucidity where I clearly saw human
beings said to be our fellow kind, such as one cannot see them
without becoming mad useless. I did see lucidity. "Why are
you killing me?" I would say. No one answered me. I was dead.
No one listened to me. In front of me people said: "what?
don't you live on the other side of the water?", as if there were
someone other than me in front of me. They were killing me,
while appearing to settle my score. "Why do you plant cacti
along my garden," I would say. What's more, they tried to
make me pay for these undesired monsters. What I see today
is that I was telling the truth, which was not and never has
been spiteful, about the assassinations of love, I saw very
clearly that these our fellow kind detest the love they claim to
love, and have not the least idea of it, all of this I showed
shown in Joyce's comedies, I was going against the – capital –
Parisian – hypocrisy in other words against the law of the
strongest, I love Proust I would say for the way he pulls back
the curtains during the pretence, the way he plunges his souls
into the mire, before witnesses, the way he loves to love love
like a pig, people would say to me: pooh. You're mad! They

couldn't say to me: it is forbidden to show the truth because officially there was only truth that was in truth lies and hypocrisy. I came "from the other side of the water," they said, but who made you judges that this side is here and that side is there? I would say. But I secretly preferred to be taken for a being from the other side with the truth on my side that they called madness and to leave on their side the usurpation become reasonable according to their illusion. My name beginning by Ci-, *Here-*, even as they sentenced me to be from There, they skinned me alive, they removed my head. They themselves wore heads that were too low on top with lipless mouths. They are right, I thought, I love madness.

Foreigner coming from a foreign land, I had discovered that all of Paris and all in Paris was shortsighted, taken up with the day-to-day, to be sure it was like that in Saint-Simon's time as well as at the time of the Restorations, I had thought it was past and gone at least in places, but everything is always shortsighted, Qohelet spoke for all time of times and each time claims that speaking without illusion is in the pluperfect, obsolete, vain, and poetic. *Thinking*, I thought, and the more I thought about it, the more I thought about thinking (I tremble when I say this word even today, still today one should never say this word without extraordinary precautions) the more I thought about thinking about thinking more the more I felt the ultra-urgent urgency of thinking about this verb this word this mission this campaign to be conducted by mobilizing all its forces, this demand for mental piety that I had believed must reign in Paris and that I had imagined was awaiting me there, probably living in the theaters suited to its development, thinking, I thought with passion and terror, is not honored, or in fashion, is not even necessary is neither considered nor valued, in particular by the visitors to the places where one might expect there to be some thinking, one can do everything without ever needing to think, from living (directing, reading, teaching philosophy, declaring war) to dying, one can totally do without it, one grants, at most one imitates, the outward appearance of thinking, one wrinkles one's brow a little one talks a lot full-throatedly,

elsewhere one forgets, one lets the moths get to it,

the profound amazement at finding Paris a machine with no curiosity then right away the fear, an impossibility of anger against any adversary because there is not even any decree, then an uneasy sorrow, the view of vision, the blind city which prevents no one from making his way with new generations of cars every five years and in fact all of these people advance, have public notoriety they are thus *right* in their idea of *thinking seriously* appearances justify them and since everywhere there are only appearances appearances are reality, all the faults are on my side.

Without lifting a little finger you break me you cover me in spit you snuff out my breath you slit the throats of my beloved animals, you cut their necks with the knife that is all the more murderous for being invisible, my animals Unconscious, Love, Thinking, Struggling, Venerating, Suffering, all butchered, skinned, plucked, simply, quickly, mechanically.

I tried to keep myself from saying these crimes I saw, I remember, I tried to clear a way for myself among the cadavers of all the noble things that might have been, I spoke to no one, everyone or almost drove around in cars over the decapitated corpses and the heads without noticing anything. Only my teacher and master glimpsed proof of what I did not say, it must have caused, I don't know, some grammatical or syntactical disturbances in my writings, moreover I wrote everything in quarters, morsels, broken columns, a morseling that J. J. disapproved of and called "contemporary influence," but it was a reverse judgment. Only once will I confide to him my horror at the fact that there seemed to be a worldwide or semi-worldwide plot against the spirit of faithfulness to the being that – I didn't want to call it genius, that is, *génie* (1) so as not to risk attracting ridicule upon this spirit (2) because the word was in any case equivocal and insufficient – I called *egien*. I saw Stendhal using these anagrammatical hiding places: *Omar* for example, he says. People thought it was *Amor*, but it was *Roma*. *A pris* was Paris, *derme merde*. On that day I interspersed my report to J. J. with English words that seemed to me stronger and less sullied than the French ones. I will quote Stendhal, to my master, as a shield, but he will reply to me that "my head is the plaything of my soul" and that my lucidity is a weakness of the brain that is not suited to women and will lead me "to the other side." In spite of which he would love me.

Around 1963 I had great need of this delirium. Madness is a protection. It stands guard against the horrors of reality. I will merely exchange one for the other when I enter the absolute love for you, in the course of my first lucidity.

I remember the principles of the First Lucidity. The person in a state of First Lucidity levitates passionately always *to the last floor*, that is to say the highest, if it's the last one in height, the ground floor if it leads to the Underground, in other words the sublime and the subliminal in the narrow buildings and peoples where the person resides. From there s/he has a duty to live always on the edge, at soul's end, leaning or perched above herself, himself and while keeping promises in a fertile and absolute manner. If s/he has to say only one word that's all.

Everything must tend toward crystal. Language is the first world. She hears very well that all words have a secret spring. Everything is worse everything is better than we think we are saying. Crystal called Christal to the above-mentioned person but one must not say so.

The person is called "person" in the charter, but the said person is otherwise free of his/her genres, species, sexes, specters, and so on. If the person keeps a journal, for example, s/he may be designated with the name "the animal." The journal and the animal are not tied or obligated to one another. Freedom is not obligated. The said person has absolute moral positions. S/he loves madly. S/he loves madness. S/he loves the mad condition. S/he loves on condition of the absolute. (That is why I turn myself over to you.) S/he may die more than once without changing lives, on the contrary, s/he will always belong to the same life, without denying unforeseen craters, bad falls, and without regretting them either.

The good reason for which I love you, that is to say the good madness, is language. It is the only one. All the rest is random.

– You could have not existed, I say and it's as if I fell a long way down into ashes

– I could not have not existed, you say.

And this is so calm, I pull myself up again.

– New York, I could not have, I could have too soon too late, in the building next door, and not have been born

Forty years increase my terror and my astonishment. I believe in God only day by day. Every day I receive a day of life. Every day I ask for the next day. The more I live the more I fear. When for the first time I read *In Search of the One Word*, I awaited from each poem the name of this word, then I reread it, each word began to be the chosen one, I began to read in the light of another word and each time it was another book, the book of another word.

You try to let be heard the word that passes in silence between the words, that is why I listen so intensely to all your words, I would like to surprise the word they are whispering among themselves. Some of them say there exists *a word*. I mean: a word that would have powers and perhaps all of them, they say. My whole life with you I have tried to find it. I have not succeeded and I am not sorry for that. For its part, it's better that it escapes me. If I found it, there would be nothing more to add. All the same I could also find it so fleetingly, so feebly that I might think I had been dreaming I would forget it immediately, I would remember only having found bliss in a joy.

In front of us there is an immense garden of words and non-words, a *serre*, that is, a greenhouse in which are preserved by my care so many things of speech you have given me while leaving me free to cultivate them.

IV

ONE TIME, AVENUE DE CHOISY

ECHO, MY LOVE

FIRST EPISODE

On Tuesday, November 12, 1993, around noon, while cross-
ing the Avenue de Choisy in Paris's 13ᵗʰ *arrondissement*, we
were coming out of the Tang Brothers' store-restaurant, I see
us, you place your right hand on my left arm to hold me back
– it's true that absorbed by my inner exultation I cast no glance
in the direction of imminent destiny – and that's when – you
say to me – at that precise moment the traffic was very dense
and energetic – I am already in the street, you barely touch me
and you say to me in French "*fais attention* mon amour," "pay
attention *my love*," I'm quite sure of it like the poor being who
is reeling from the telephone call from God is sure of God
whose face he does not see – I didn't see you you are a little
behind me, a half-step – but the being is not and will never be
sure of itself, it believes indeed that the one it calls God said
to him: my love – pay attention to what you're doing, but it
would not swear to that, and it is structurally inconceivable for
the being to say "What?", one doesn't ask God to repeat him-
self, God speaks only once, when he says the same thing twice

it's because he's angry, it seems to me and I believe indeed that
you said these words but I will never swear to it (1) because
there is and must be a doubt (2) because it would be mean,
vulgar, illegitimate contrary to want to notarize words of a
free, musical, divine species, of an invisible and fabulous bird
that the violinist lets rise out of his own body the world stag-
gered, I am sure of that, at that very instant I became a woman
from another world but undeclared, but invisible, but on the
edge of which I remained, amazed and incredulous

We were crossing, was I distracted, the traffic was brutal,
we were naturally occupied with avoiding being thrown under
the wheels of a car, a frequent accident in this neighborhood
where one passes within a hair's breadth of death every day,
and indeed at the moment you uttered these few words a foot
away from my shoulder, one of these monstrous vehicles
roared past grazing my body, then nothing more than your
words, as astounding in this landscape as an orchard in the
middle of a battlefield.

Then we were on the other side.

I was burning with uncertainty. I was sure I had heard your
phrase end with the expression "my love" in French. I was not
sure you had said these words, they could have slipped out,
hadn't we been in life for more than thirty years without your
having ever uttered these two words, or any equivalent or syn-
onym, so they would have come by chance, from no one
knows where, to hook themselves onto your warning phrase,
but I have never heard you make a *faux pas*, all the same the
words were uttered I say to myself, we were going back up the
avenue side by side, breathing with the ease that is the sign of
habit, without either insistence or emphasis, they seemed to
come back for the thousandth time with the innocence of
familiarity, I couldn't think therefore that you might have said
them expressly, they would have borne the weight of inten-
tion, whereas these words that were said or that you said for

the first time absolutely had every appearance of notes that
were not thinking about it, they were gentle and tamed, they
were laughing, careless, without consciousness, I mused, or
else no, they had not escaped you, you had indeed said them,
but as if you had first unburdened them of a gravity accumu-
lated by the past years without any convocation, in the
unknown reserve where numerous subjects of silence live a life
that we never know anything about. Perhaps moreover they
had never resided with the unsaid things? Perhaps they had
never been either captives or under spiritual control? Perhaps
they had just been *born*? Had I become mylove that very day?
And since they had just for the first time come to land on your
lips they had that childish look of a first smile. I had a thou-
sand questions to ask you, which I would not have asked you
under any circumstances. There had perhaps been a careless
mistake? Or a giddiness of the heart? I had heard speak of
oaths sworn also in a story, it was Fouqué's *Undine*, one must
not say certain things on pain of destruction of the world, can
life depend on an unshared secret? But that was German
romanticism, and the strange being who cannot say and who
is on the other side of the water is she. Or else we are an
inverse version, you are the Undin under oath, I'm the one
who talks all the time and understands nothing. But I'm the
one on Avenue de Choisy who is inundated and says not a
word. And why, in the street, between two torrents of murder-
wielding cars, in the awful din, I might not have heard them,
I almost didn't, we were swimming, my mouth was full of
water.

Or else you were waiting for the moment, their moment, to
let them loose, without having ever been able to foresee which
moment that would be, where it would happen? It would be a
no-matter-where that would forever after become holy and
nameable by the name of the words or of the place like one of
God's rocks in the desert. The place would thereby join

Olivier de Serres in the group of consecrated places remark-
able by their modest and accidental aspect that form a more
literary ensemble. It would have been attributed to us by the
will of fate. We were heading toward the car. I see you say
clearly: "We'll come back." You half-turn round toward the
restaurant. Where will we come back? When? Why? Are you
thinking of a celebration? An evocation? The Chinese menu?
  Perhaps, I thought, you wanted to have said without saying
once, a single time? And so as to be able to say without saying,
or to be able to have said, it was perhaps necessary not to have
said those words and for years and years and years until there
would have certainly disappeared from our soul any trace
memory expectation virtuality of possibility of ever desiring
or imagining the coming of these words or similar words so as
to have reached with certainty another time like another
planet where never yet would these words have taken flight, in
order that these words, so ancient worn said by two million
people at the same time once every half-hour, be like found-
words. I would have passionately wished to be sure, at the
moment we approached the sidewalk, that you had *said* these
words, at least that, that they were *from* you and not *by* you,
distractedly, and that they were not the opposite of what I
hoped they were. But I showed nothing. I realize that my ver-
tigo and my instinct caused me to imitate the innocence your
face maintained in the sweet grip of the dream, I walk, I see
myself walking as if I had heard nothing, whereas I would like
to fall on the ground and weep. I think: because of the history
of possessives in French, *mon* of *monamour* can designate the
other or oneself. If you say *mon amour*, it's the question that
disturbs this *mon*, perhaps it's not me, possessives have this
strange ability to indicate possession and identity, *or* identity,
I see Baudelaire saying my beauty to the beggar woman, he's
talking however perhaps about his own beauty, I torment
myself, it's a delight, such a common expression for a unique

or rare feeling, it's a tragedy, one can even say my love without any love. "I love you" I say to myself, that you would never say, I say to myself it's a declaration, it would go against all your poetic work, I don't see the one from the mountain saying that to his servant, for he does not have to say it, and mylove neither moreover, never any my. At moments I was on the verge of persuading myself I had imagined these words. It then became still more unthinkable for me to ask you if you had said them.

That I am for you or with you, there is not the least doubt for me. But that I am yours, that is something else, you would still have to want to be the owner. And now that was said. And why? Now there was all the time before this Tuesday in November. All times have changed name and significance. Or else it was for having said it once so as to give a name to all the years that now were past? I never knew never thought.

Now you had said it one time. Perhaps there will never be but one time? Only one day?

What is one time? It is so alone, so glorious, so disturbing so radiant. It was still there, in the street.

One might say mylove without saying my love? I thought. You would have done that? It would be superhuman, it would be you. It would not be me, me I say to you my love, it's true I must have begun rather late in our story: I was afraid of four kinds of violence (1) possessive violence (2) the latter can become predatory violence if one is not careful (3) the violence of erosion (4) the violence of almost lying without doing so on purpose. Because the mylove can become a kind of proper name; a permanent pilot light that has nothing more in common with the Cry.

I believe I have not betrayed. Under my breath or aloud I have always cried out, I believe. I call you. You are walking next to me, suddenly, it's necessary, I call you. It's as if your presence right next to me were so strong that I physically felt from shoulder to hip, to thigh, down to my feet the open wound of the separation of skins, bloods, nerves as if I remembered in my flesh having been cut off from you, you were sleeping then, but as for me I was not asleep, I still feel the shears, I cry out asking you for forgiveness if it caused you pain. My soul does everything it can to repair the irreparable.

If I consider my host country, literature, it is rare that one has recourse to the expression itself, moreover most often one meets up only with third persons, the fire is under glass, people make love only once every five hundred pages, except in *The Desert of Passion*. That's always the problem: literary writers – of which I am one – need to talk, in order to talk. Sometimes one needs not to say in order to say. But all those who write cannot be poets. I am one of those who write.

Now we are driving toward the Porte d'Italie.

– Will we come back to the source of words?

I was sure that we would never come back.

Then: does *one* time exist? What does one time mean? One time is almost a Never. Perhaps there would not even be a Never if there were not one time an incomprehensible notch in the heart of time. A second's rest. I stopwatch "monamour." It takes exactly a second.

Today am I the heir of 12.11.93? Do I have a crown? Do you know what happened on 12.11.93? Were you there? There was no famous monument in the neighborhood. There was no gathering. No uprising of a crowd or of indignation. Will I still remember this day for a long time? Without ever speaking to you about it? How to speak to you? How would I never speak to you about it?

Thirty years you say have gone by *Commeça*, Likethat, but one might also say fifty years or sixty years, there are no years in the alliance, years Likethat add up to a livingbeing that extends to different parts of the Universe. We are more and more cities at the outset we were only Paris and New York I'm not counting Algiers that I had left

To say, I say to myself, that it's in Paris, a city that has never loved us, that the invisible alliance took place. Will I alone remember this day for a long time yet? Perhaps there exists a version of 12.11.93 in your archives? Perhaps in your own memory you visit this place saying to yourself that on 12.11.93 you said to me and I said nothing, as if I had heard nothing, as if I had heard without understanding or understood without hearing, as if I had been a little absent, a little distracted, a little deaf as if I were sleeping when our earth quaked, perhaps there exists another version of 12.11.93 about which I have no idea, perhaps in that version you are thinking of the solitude that unites two solitudes that understand one another so well. Or perhaps you say to yourself that I heard correctly and correctly I said nothing, that I responded with correct distraction to these words that are extremely serious. Naturally there is no way you could ask me if I had indeed heard. Perhaps when you visit this day you murmur in passing an image of Avenue de Choisy: I hope.

Getting older I fear that the apparatus of recollection is no longer in good working order, in the same order, I fear that a grain of doubt troubles my view, I fear that by covering itself over in time the day of 12.11.93 begins to look like a dream. That it has the fragile clarity, the trembling visual substance of a dreamed event. I never pass by Avenue de Choisy anymore. What if I foundered there? I could not go there alone, the risk of collapse is too great. I could go there only with you. I could go there with you only if chance led us there. I can't see myself saying to you: how about if we go to Avenue de Choisy? You would look at me with that face of incomparable innocence that you put on whenever you sense, in an animal fashion, that there is in a sentence I advance in your direction something hidden behind the words, you sniff it, you probe it, you would say to me in a voice slightly bristling with curiosity: Avenue de Choisy? And everything would be forever lost, I would be disinherited, I would be deposed, I would be bent over with shame. Thereupon you add: Why? Worse, you say: If you want. Each one of your words, each sweet inflection of your docile voice digs the grave deeper deeper, something dies, I cannot lament. But perhaps you say to me: Avenue de Choisy? in a veiled voice, you have several of them that I know, that I absolutely cannot interpret, is it connivance? are you nearing the marvelous rock of the covenant with the same supernatural delicacy as in the past, renewing here and now the *as if it were nothing* of 12.11.93? And for my feverish brain everything starts up again, the cloudy mystery, the sojourn in another zone, where all the signs speak in another, superior language, a language that speaks above and beneath words through reflections through glimmers through pauses where it is the commas that indicate *with their absence* the path that thought has to follow eyes closed, a language that speaks voices the words are the somewhat crude supports of celestial music. It's as if we earthlings had to climb up on stools to bring our ear close to the beatings of the air.

I can't resolve to take the risk of the proposal. I see my cowardice, I stick to it. We did not return to Avenue de Choisy. That means nothing. There is time. We never have time, neither of us. We do have time to spend a day at Avenue de Choisy, it will happen perhaps, ten years is nothing either.

There are three kinds of places of events. The places to which we return. The interval varies from several months to several years. The places to which we have never returned as real beings but to which we return often as spirits and with a happiness of believers. These are places endowed with a very great memorial intensity in themselves, adorable and rare places that seem to benefit from a magic privilege because they have survived every attack for hundreds of years, the wars of religion being powerless against their incarnation. The places that seem to have been destined to a non-return, to which it would be possible to return without material effort and that are maintained as impossible. I could make lists of them.

Avenue de Choisy constitutes in itself a fourth species. In me 12.11.93 secretly aspires to prolong itself until the incredible day when I would dare to speak to you of it. Between my life and this scene there is an attachment of flesh. I would lose one of our children if I lost it. And yet.

Or else you choose to say these words in a non-place, between two shores, in the moving and steep interval between launched vehicles, perhaps you were even looking for that occasion, with no relation to the stability of the divan or the bed, or else you were looking for the moment of a street name bearer of a meaning that is at once obvious and a little dissimulated; or else it's the anxiety that grabbed hold of you on seeing me cross blindly which projected you into another scene, altogether virtual, where having lost me through the most improbable of accidents you realize with me having disappeared and only then that you loved me without having had the possibility or the chance of being informed of that during my lifetime, as is the case for the majority of mortals. In an instant, a second suffices, you will have seen the terrible night you spend the day after that day that no one expects in reality even while expecting it all the time in the cruel games of imagination, the day whose endless suffering the narrator tried to convey to us when he had lost Albertine for the second time, an event so extraordinary, so improbable, so unbelievable that no reader refuses to believe it for a second precisely because it is totally unbelievable and it escapes, by virtue of its irrational, monstrous, unruly aspect, all evaluation, all opinion, this accident that makes a mockery of everything is a satan that's its appalling force, one is summoned to believe the unbelievable and while vacillating one believes it, abandoning all equilibrium, one falls into the hole dug out in reason, one doesn't hang onto the edge, there is none, one is carried off, a horse stands up beneath our weight, and with a gigantic kick throws us beneath the wheels of the chariot passing by right at that very moment. All of this mad horror will have taken the time of a comma in a sentence. In the shock caused by this infernal image you will have lost these words, they will have rolled into the street, at once posthumous and precipitous, then you will have awakened from the descent into the Inferno beside me, in the process of crossing Avenue de Choisy, with these escaped words at your side.

I had never thought of the powers of the name of this avenue before today. Everyone knows that the occult powers of the decisive things in our lives are immense and when they decide us for death it is immeasurable, but this knowledge is fearful, holed up, easily intimidated, especially the power of places-things that is a veritable plot by the gods, personally I have nothing to fear or to draw from the Champs-Élysées but Proust who carried this avenue with all its strollers was himself hell incarnate in a human phial, and how could Julien Sorel and Mme de Rênal not have been brought to the boil in their Verrières, a late addition to Dante's damned "I might have married such a man" she cried out to her feverish dream and he who said to himself "anyway, it's not going to last a lifetime, this madness," would he ever have adored her like a battle to be waged if they had not followed blindly the Cours de la Fidélité, Fidelity's Way, whose plane trees are razed to the bone by a barbaric authority manipulated in secret by the demons of destiny. An avenue, a mayor, a gardener's puppet hand would turn these magnificent lovers into vulgar kitchen garden plants with low flat and rounded heads if on the contrary they didn't push them in the direction of revolution. Will we ever know who, what power in us in you bearing me on you in me altogether haunted by you, will have chosen and why, that day, that year, Avenue de Choisy, to cause us to pass by there, or to make us say or pass or carry there that message this time and no other time, the first and the last, whether by annunciation or by denunciation, instantly immensely faithful and tenuous of our fleeting promenage through the eternities? Who, hidden, will have *passed on* this message? Will I ever be able to say I received it? I let it pass by, an event superior to me, let it go and land on the flexible tip of a twig of one of the neighborhood's acacias, dense small invisible except for the wide swaying of the whole branch that such a light body causes. In retrospect this being of words looked exactly like those marvelous animals that my dream factory invents each time in just one copy, so unique and mad that it demands and defies description. Like that person-being I met this morning on the landing, a lady, my neighbor in truth, no bigger than an arm, whose body is indistinguishable from her head in a sheath of canary yellow feathers, a little timid, but dignified, and whom I thought I should congratulate on her successful appearance. A combination of fish and bird. What will I say about this mylove? It tickled and stuttered, it was the name and the song of a delicate species. I would have liked to be from another kingdom at that instant, speak another language.

Why didn't you say this *thing* to me in a café? For example our New York café. Or the Japanese tea room. Or our restaurant at the Cathedral, or another. Seated face to face, or side by side, while we studied the menus of our faces? I could cite thousands of superb little scenes, with or without view on the universe. I well understand that all this That will have taken place precisely no place in particular and will not have been able to take place in a fixed place, or even a human one. A voice on a path, *une voix sur une voie*, that's your signature.

One could say sixty years one hundred and sixty years less sixty years, years like That grow in the corners of the Garden of Times, they are behind the fence I pass along the fence, you are on the other side of the fence you are on high, you are in your office with a poem that is your master, and with the numeral of which I am the repeat, the office is an inside one without a window, a nest in the rock of the world, there is always a nest, no one either friend or enemy can put his face in an opening, never any glass-*verrière*, I walk along the fence of Fidelity, are we inside are we outside, a hundred times I go back up the street, my heart pounding, what if I were to find you! what if I were not to find you! it starts over and continues, one can't bear the beauty of time that goes back up, goes down and goes back up and goes by like That while we remain, remainder of time, without the help of the Safeguards. At night, seeing time that passes in counted hours, seeing the end of the night coming and the end of time, seeing that I haven't written, that I haven't packed my bags, seeing that I didn't hear you that day, I cry out loud into the disarray of the house: help! help! at night especially for that's when I *see* time *passing* I bleed, I lose every minute, an awful bleeding of time that makes me yell: help! help! I call all the forces that help one respond to the draining away. I must keep what is passing. Help! my friends! my notebooks! my desks! my telephones! I don't want to lose this day, I don't want it to pass and to have passed into nothingness. Come to my aid! This day has a name, a life, it's a child, I don't want it to die. Every day I spend time keeping time, I photograph, I fortify, I record, I whip-stitch, I save, I pass along the fence, I pick a leaf of ivy, I begin time again, I breathe double, this lasts a year at the beginning and right away after that ten years and me telling everything. How many leaves have I picked and kept. It takes so little space all this time. The vast staircases of stone that lead to your nest. In 1965, I can be seen climbing them very quickly, in 1975 I put my foot on the first step in 1985 my life and I go up in 1995 in glass armor, at the least shock it breaks: a certain accent of the voice, the vicinity of two words. Continue, you say. I continue. In 2005 I put the word: *continue* in the word drawer.

I am writing along the fence.

I see time, its work, on my mother the great Goddess we are walking along the beach in 2005, her arm hooked in my arm, she has gotten frail this year her right side leans, the cane-umbrella on the other side, the great Goddess cries out: what are you writing up there? I cry out: a kind of love story. She cries out: it's like the sea, it goes, it comes.

– Turn around, I cried. I stick a post-it on the tablet of her back. I note. The little sheet stuck onto the docile back of time.

I note: "*Ça va*," it goes, it's OK. The *Ça va* is not OK at all.

V

FIRST LETTERS

On Monday, July 12, 2003, I was in a plane (from A to B) as if I were not there: I was with the first letters, all your letters to you to me for the first time since the first time, a madness, a necessity, it's the first time they have gone out, that I have gone out with them, if the plane falls, if I die with the letters –

I was with them with you I went from them to you, I was trembling all over, I recognized them, I didn't recognize them, all these letters that are the cause, these paper tablets size 148 cm x 210 cm, you used paper the color of your skin, it was not paper already your hand I was touching the touch of your hand, I felt the touch of your hand touch the paper that I was then touching I don't remember how anymore I think my fingers must have been slightly uneasy at present my fingers my eye-fingers my lip-fingers all my soul's caressed tactile extremities were caressing the incessant trembling of the paper, there is no material that so strangely faithfully so faithfulstrangely keeps the trace of breathless emotions in the limbs of the words, the legs feet necks chest of the words expressed on every line were still and for always quivering with what you were – was he – was it – were you you already before me – or else on contact with the paper

– and almost all of them ended with the word: faithfully, *fidèlement* in French (I saw this at a very quick glance when opening the envelope and taking up with one hand fifteen letters not one of which would have ever thought either to be followed by other letters or many other letters or of being one day much later still living crying diaphanously in my hands the same ones but more anxious more timid more sensitive to the touch)

or else on contact with the paper that senses in advance, that lends itself, that mute already knows what its mission will be to bear, because the paper is your forerunner, it is for you what the ass is for Abraham, it has to be your ass, there has to be the ass first of all and before who consents to and aids everything you are going to notsay while painfully climbing up your reticent slope,

– I look at this barely rugged and soft paper, it already knew, as soon as you placed the palm of your left hand on its flank, as soon as you bent the pen toward its neck, I see it reading with its whole body the effort and the fright, it is the first the humble superalert one, who hears the rustling of the sentence that you will not say, the stifling of breath between your teeth, it is the paper ass that will have been the first to know what was coming down on you, the shawl of silence around each bloody word, the order of march forward backward, the unavowable upheaval necessarily of all the sorts of fears, dreads, apprehensions, anxieties, pangs, disturbances, frights but without straying, alarm, confusion, it's he I see the magnanimous mount of your conflicting passions, the first confidant of the torment that peoples you with opposing temptations, you take the bit in your mouth and you spur it on, I look at the first witness of your solitude,

I am in the plane as if I were above the clouds at the height of your interior mountain – seeing you then I would never have suspected it – climbing toward vertigo – were you *you* already before this paper, born-climber perhaps destined to the service of the abyss and already under orders – or else on contact with the paper that you dispatched to me, you had just received – no – you were receiving the intimation of this you that you might happen to be,

I was in a state of eternal agitation with them
and almost all of them ended with the word: *fidèlement*
Such a word, in French, in your mouth,
It was a prayer, a wish in the storm
A sad and sorry word a word unfaithful to itself a synonym of synonym: voluntarily, involuntarily fearfully with courage oh if only I could be me, oh if only I knew how to be me signed: *fuidèlement*, flightfully.

I read this word in the plane where I am as if I were not there, such a word, the plane nosedives, my last breath will have been your name but how will anyone know this, how will you know that I have been faithful unto death, you alone you can be faithful to the idea of my absolute fidelity,

such a word – in your mouth – I don't recall what it said to me, I remember thoughts of my mouth around your tongue, I remember what I thought of your tongue, my reverent fear of your tongue plunged down to the hilt but I don't remember my thoughts around the sword of this word. Was I who I would be? No doubt I began under your frightened laws. I know I doubted the meaning of your word that I obeyed to the letter. I didn't understand your injunctions, I tried to understand the two sides of them and their shadow. I was with you, it seems to me that we were together, and surely we were but how, the long broken uneven paths beaten by immoderate seasons, I followed you, where are we going? you cried, I followed you you were in front of me how could I have answered you with a word, we are going where, I thought, what I could assert is that since I was following you closely – I read you, I was at the distance of reading, every step, every poem, read – you didn't risk falling backwards.

You, when you signed faithfully *fidèlement*, you who were already you in poem, you knew what you were doing by sending me this word without any doubt, but did you know what this word did to me? *Fidèle ment*, faithful lies.

I must have circled around this word, with fright and attraction I must have tried to inhale its aura with the tips of my moustaches, the cat that I was by my carnal need and cautiousness, I must have wanted not to hesitate to – but to what?

But perhaps you didn't know anything you didn't think anything, perhaps you were yourself preceded by a word that was stronger and more rapid than your hypnotized being, perhaps you were following it?

How I love you today as in the times of Virgil and Ovid times before times after how I love you for having loved you straight ahead on a bias crossways along every path I was as if at home in the exile of your words

And to have seen you so little finally and to have read you day and night and to have seen you so often in dreams, in such diverse lives, like that night when *for the first time* we were together in Algiers. "I was in the streets with you, I didn't remember any name, I was in the state of a birth, I went with you, I raised my head, I inhaled, you smell that? I didn't smell anything, it didn't smell like anything, oh well that doesn't matter, it was Algiers. Algiers I cried very loud. Algiers! I was crying out, you were laughing. This word had incredible powers!" This time if you ask me where are we going? I tell you: to Algiers. And you follow me.

We know all about the joys of exile.

What was I doing reading, without reading them exactly, looking at the faces and the features of the being, the letter

that you were in the past in an ancient time that is our neigh-
bor? All the words you no longer say. The word: *fidèlement*,
you no longer say it to me, it's been impossible for us for a long
time, I say. "A long time"? you say
   – I mean, I say, that as soon as the word *fidèlement* was
crossed off our tablets the very-long time began. But I don't
know the date on which you crossed it off.

VI

NOTEBOOK LIFE

There are the notebooks. They have their habits.

I don't know why I note down everything. Everything? It cannot be otherwise. Everything that I am apt to note down: everything that happens every day to one of us and that I can translate. Everything that is woven between us, and everything that is in preparation. Sometimes I am tired. For example for dreams. A voice whispers: don't note it. I am tempted. I note it anyway. I obey. The notebook. It's not fine work. I paint crudely. I follow the trail.

The notebook is my third cat. It is always on my desk with the other two. My paper cat. When a notebook is done I deposit it in a greenhouse. Right away it enters another time. It has been closer to me than anyone for a year. It knows us better than I – this year. Now: forgotten, it remembers, in secret. It sleeps, in no order, it keeps watch without orders. It falls into an unvisited memory.

I said: everything. But there is on the other side everything that is not in the notebooks. Everything that doesn't go in there, can't. Won't? The notebook, the spirit of the notebook, me perhaps. There are all those wild leaves that do not go in, that keep to themselves. They will be found in a drawer, but not under the cover, not under the roof. They are large leaves and incompatible with the music of the notebooks. They look like struggles, dry humors, moments of shame difficult to explain, embarrassed or embarrassing. Like defects, who exactly their author is one doesn't know. Their presence outside the notebooks deserves a two-part analysis. As I see it (I am thinking about this today for the first time), the notebooks form the thread, the wild leaves: the cut. Or else the body and the notch. Or as if there were an indecency that the specific essence of the notebook didn't accept or that didn't accept to be mixed with the generally delightful tone of the notebooks, if one asks me why or for whom I keep these notebooks, I feel that I cannot answer clearly. I do not read them myself. No one reads them. I have been given the duty, I don't know by whom.

Then what? What a difference between the appearance of the wild pages and that of the notebook pages! On the large sheets everything is disjunction, altercation, everything has large features, there are large blanks between slender paragraphs, the sentences are broken, unfinished, beaten, the limbs cut off any which way, many crossings-out, sometimes two words then one word on a line, you can see there is a sort of stampeding of the breathless movements that take up half a page, everything points to disorder, hurried escape: there's not a second to spare, it's cut and run. The danger must be extremely close, no time to finish a word. Let's be off. We'll see later if there is a later. The notebooks: completely the opposite. The writing is dense, small, crowded, the space is entirely occupied, it's because one is trying to fill up the suitcase or the box to the maximum, one might have to carry it out if there's an attack or a fire, time is piled up, they are trunks, stores.

The others: epilepsies. One can see the crises, the body is rolled up against the furniture, the tongue twisted back. With the notebooks, you could want to read them. You could read them. The leaves fear you. They are afraid. They are so afraid that I don't even know of what.

In truth they are fear itself. Its faces, its flights, its solitudes. I myself flee them. I cut off their speech. But I don't destroy the stump.

They are masked when they surge onto my scene. For a few instants, the time it takes to mingle and interfere with me. And always like madwomen who have leapt out of bed unwashed uncombed, bandages on their feet, bare-breasted like young widowed women accused of adultery with monsters of ugliness and nastiness, dragged to the pyre of the ordeal on which they hasten to throw themselves to put an end as quickly as possible to the visions of horror by asphyxiating first because that is expedient. They tell me they are called Littegarde a name they take from a character in a narrative by Kleist whose fate is such a perfection of horror-happiness that her story has always made me heartsore before the end. Littegarde or Lettergarde I think or Littergarde. I'm sure of "garde." Everything accuses them, they can't prove anything, they only want to die, eyes caved in, heart broken. Once, twice perhaps, I dreamed that I was as if caved in all over all the people who love me one after the other condemned my being and betrayed me in front of me, on top of everything I was accused of defending myself and of crying out. Perhaps these fits were in truth dreams that had drifted into day. They would have gone to the wrong theater. The panicked ones had arrived from a foreign theater, they had gotten off at the wrong station, they were already or still acting in a play that I could have written in the Middle Ages, I don't deny it, but certainly not in our time. They would belong to a repertory from *before*, it could go back to the age of caves, my own. That would explain why I can neither recognize them nor disown them. The Littegardes would perhaps be the subjects of the Underside come from the other side of my mirror, mental illnesses of the sort suffered in locked-up states? It sometimes happens that my brain is encircled and trampled by bad thoughts but I take an anti-inflammatory and then they are dispelled. The Littegardes are unpredictable, they suddenly swoop down on the skull, they perforate the walls and the years, they drive in nails, they make holes, I knew their terrors during my first lucidity, they are unbearable to listen to, one wants to die, they pass, one is resuscitated, one doesn't think about them anymore at all for ten years.

The notebooks are innumerable, there are some in every locked drawer in the house, they make up an adorable, chaotic population. It is my tribe. Material for writing? No. There is no use. Then what use? I don't see. The notebook is an obligation. Has always been? When did we begin? I could root around in the drawers. These animals are all different: their bodies are small square fat large long thick paltry heavy very small, equally loved, naturally, the way one adopts animal love. Their life is rather short but regularly ardent.

At the time of my first lucidity your words came upon me like showers of light, moreover I didn't think you spoke to me or even that you spoke, it seemed to me that you made light, you said little, each verse undid a shadow in front of me, you didn't speak, you split open, each sentence was an event of thinking to be thought, before I had never heard thinking that is to say doing that is to say stirring up it seems to me that it seemed to me I was hearing seeing doing for the first time, I was amazed, me whose days had been lowered into the bowels of the subway, I was afraid of falling under the ground and being pocketed again, I have the impression that I began running in your wake, from the second day I picked up everything, fetuses, bits of wood, pearls, I was afraid of losing the pearls of light as the hundred plays of Aeschylus were lost. As soon as I gathered them, however small and however short, your sentences began to make a world for me, but a world as yet never said. It's a question of world: when there is one that begins to be assembled one can no longer renounce it. Montaigne as well I do not think of renouncing him. He is one of my vestiges, one of the vital organs of my person. Moses as well can't renounce the tablets that are speaking in his chest, one cannot get along without lungs.

If you were going to leave, there would remain for a world all that I had gathered.

But there are very few wild leaves

I have always been afraid. What happiness you have known say the notebooks. And it is always there, in the drawers. You have always known such fear and Fear. Fear of not lasting fear of lasting. Pure fear, fear of fear, fear against fear, flames of joy, joys of fear. This word *fidèlement* right away, what a shiver. It's your fear that made me afraid. And it is still there.

Did I wish to know the furniture in your room? The idea never occurred to me. Your home? Your entourage? I didn't think of that. I was completely absorbed by your poem, attached to your page. I would have liked to be able to have seen the birth of this – speaking – body, to have received it as it left the god, so as to lose nothing of the miracle, I was enthused by perfection, all the elements of your language that began to say, together and separately such poignant things, it is life in death the being we would like to embrace and save in the book, the speech of commas, the humble and powerful love of sin without regret without punctuation, the enjamb-ment that changes everything one thinks it's finished it comes to life again a blank later what a lesson and each time, instantly eyes blindfolded it's thus my last minute, I want to think,

I think nothing, three words later restored to life, oh how everything happens in a half-page threat powerlessness mourning resurrection, and the mocking articles the speech of sounds, the faraway sobbings
    it is worth all the pain of living
    but what pain also in reading, one must climb
    the mountain proposes an edge, always
    you stretch out your hand or it's a branch of words
    once across the first step I know it the mountain will lift me up to its head,
    but in front of the first parapet I get weak: I cannot lift my leg I have to take my leg in my two hands and hoist it onto the ledge. Before some outsiders I explain this maneuver, I'm afraid of ruining my lovely stockings I say. But before you, I joyfully confess my weakness. I am lightning-struck. I have the weight of the infinite on me. Raise me up. Place me on your lip. Each time you raise me above myself. I take strength from your strength. Once the impossibility is past, I've been reprieved I stand up naturally, the heights receive me
    – But the poems do not explain themselves, they love themselves, I tell you. You're on the telephone. You belong to this world that calls. We call ourselves, one another. All the time. We recall ourselves, one another. Ours is another world.
    – *Nos poèmes*, our poems, you say. *Nos peaux aiment*, our skins love.
    And to see one another so little in sum "in reality" is to seek to see and meet one another constantly in the second reality. Rarity gives: poems.

I said that there was no one besides god in the first desert Olivier de Serres.
    Much later came the witnesses. It is thought at first that they are cats, they are unwanted, I don't want more love. But

it's god in the bedroom, one cannot not receive the envoys one cannot not receive the poems.

You write *Two Witnesses*. Two is witness. No one knows who is the witness of whom. Two is witness[4]

We can no longer live without them. Yet there was a time without cats. But perhaps we were then the before-cats of the cats.

– Reread the Apocalypse.

– I open and I find our cats. "These are *the two olive trees* and the two torches standing *before the Lord of the earth*." These cats who are Temple olive trees have every power, the power of fire, the power to devour, the power of water the power of blood the power to open and the power to close, the power to die before we do and the power to be put back on their feet when we suffer too much from their absence.

All is written. It is written that the cat will die before I do. I don't want any dying and yet dyings happen to us, as cats we die, we die alive, it is a suffering of an abominable purity and yet we can no longer live without cats without olive trees, we lose life, the sky is closed, not a word can be spoken for months. We die. To die is also a power. The cats come back. Our cats are now called Philia and Aletheia.

I went back down. When we come back down from god, we eat, "give me to eat" you say – I give-you-to-eat, you eat what I give-you-to-eat I eat what I give-you-to-eat. We eat some given-salmon.

We eat ourselves, one another a little, gently, not yet.

– Shall I give you to eat?

– Not to the others.

To mix loving and eating, loveating, gives the love of cats.

---

[4] This repeated phrase, "Deux est témoin," is a close echo of "Dieu est témoin," "God is witness." (Tr)

The cats eat near us, at the same time as us, the same time as us mixed

The Frenchman eats dates. They are especially good. He will remember the dates. By melting their young fresh ripe flesh in his mouth they take him from a dark despair to an almost mad joy. The day before was September 22, 1798, he was going to kill himself. He saw the dates at just that moment.

My notebooks are full of dates. If I were going to kill myself some day, all I would need to do is open one of these baskets, I would find there the eternally young ripe fresh manna, I would suck the sugar of one of our days and I would be taken suddenly from despair to a somewhat somber joy. We need dates to eat, food for the heart.

– I will always remember that marvelous *Fettkugel* that was so good and so greasy says my mother, I had invited one day in Algiers two friends one of whom was mine who wanted to know what it was. One must eat the *Fettkugel* very hot and very little. They ate too much and they were both sick. Eating in small quantity, says my mother.

– There are devouring passions, I say. *The Red and the Black*, I devour. *The Idiot. Cousin Pons* is so beautiful I can't finish it. The day after Omi died, her daughter my mother went to do her marketing. My mother is the simplest form of the taste of living.

Omi my grandmother was the author of the *Gefühltekuchen*, a cake rolled in chapters, on the subject of which you said to me one day when we were eating, eating thus Germany, literature, Strasbourg Cathedral right next to which was the bakery where Omi bought beer yeast in 1910, that "When it comes to erotic reserve, the Mona Lisa is nothing at all next to this."

– That makes me think, the *Fettkugel* says my mother. It reminds me of the culinary trip that I didn't want to make. That Mr Hagenauer who was so fat and flabby had invited me to make a long culinary trip. I think he had always been a butcher, is that just my imagination, this big fat guy had been in a concentration camp and when he came back he weighed no more than seventy pounds. He gained it back. He was as fat after as before. But before this after he met when he came out of the camp a charming witty woman whom he married weighing seventy pounds (and who didn't have children having been sterilized). It was a lean marriage apparently. When he gained it back she had an affair with her brother-in-law M. Füld an intelligent and slender, distinguished man who had founded in Algeria a canned-food factory that he called *Dea*. Dea was the name people gave to the sister-in-law. His wife Mrs Füld was corpulent and educated she was the sister of the fat Mr Hagenauer. At the time of the events they left for Carpentras and they began a new *Dea* factory. Mr Füld had said to his wife who didn't know how to drive says my mother and who gave him lots of useless advice: you are *imbuvable*.[5] I didn't know this word *imbuvable* at the time. I am a gossip says my mother. It's this word *imbuvable* that interested me. One day I was visiting Carpentras, I was rather surprised to see that Mr Füld didn't open his mouth. I understood that he had Alzheimer's. After, his wife, corpulent Charlotte stayed alone with her still fat brother whose charming wife Dea had died. Dea was slenderness itself, she was seductive.

She used to talk to me about her ovaries, she showed me the lines of scars on her belly, she undertook my sentimental education, I was ten years old, she wore make-up, her enormous green eyes her large mouth, her husky voice, she used to show

---

[5] Unbearable, but literally, undrinkable. (Tr)

me the tattooed number on her skinny arm, she enchanted
me, I say, I ate asparagus I say, there were Dea canned goods
spiny lobster with mayonnaise I say, I used to eat Dea laugh-
ing then there was ice cream, I was intoxicated I had never
eaten lobster then there was the brillat-savarin pastry, she had
tanned bare arms, bracelets on her wrists, I remember her
aqua dress, this woman was sex, all the more erotic that she
was sterilized I watched her shine and I ate, I all-swallowing I
was drunk on lobster, on visions of hell, Mr Hagenauer
showed me his fat hands, they had cut off two of his fingers, it
was like meat, he also had a tattooed number, he worked in the
mines an SS officer used to slip him in secret the peels of the
apple he was eating, the peels saved him, I swallowed ladles of
mayonnaise, Dea's round thin little legs and at the end little
feet in high-heeled golden sandals then I went back up to the
knees, up to the belly where there were not her ovaries I swal-
lowed the pink ice cream with the asparagus I was endless she
loved me she hugged me I expected to see her naked beneath
a long emerald-green shawl, the jewels also naked, then I
began to feel the earth rise up and turn round on me the term
concentration camp clenched my forehead, I couldn't hold
myself in my chair or standing I saw my heart big as a crab
scurry over the green wall, I was sobbing from this disheart-
ening nausea, I was on the big bed at my paternal grand-
mother's as if I was going to die the bed rolled so much to one
side that I couldn't keep my head in front of me it fell over
between my thighs my grandmother herself was a rock if only
I could hang on to her but my hands were sticky with a
mayonnaise of vomited icecreamlobsterasparagus on the
other side my maternal grandmother had a washcloth,
between the two there was a hole between Dea's table and the
bed, the entrance to the mine, a white crater, between my
two grandmothers I was possessed by lobster by sex by the
asparagus the call of fat the call of lean and the knife blows of

the camp in the belly Dea luxury preserve, it's indigestion says my paternal grandmother we don't know that says my maternal grandmother how charming is death I thought when it comes in a green veil that graceful insect emanating from the mines with its large mouth that snatches the air and breathes plague into my stomach

she was very charming says my mother, Dea still exists, but not she, her husband still very fat had invited me on the Culinary Trip to stop at nice hotels eat well read every evening the menus for tomorrow, I'm not fond of these sensual pleasures I say, says my mother, I decline the offer, it was not my style says my mother, visiting museums yes traveling for the stomach doesn't interest me. Bad luck that the two big eaters were brother and sister, two fat people well suited to understand each other but with a mistake that was the end. I loved. I thought. I loved this simplified woman who survived those scars. Those? Her? Those. I loved – the scars. Dea preserves. A flag and on it the arms of Dea: necklaces trinkets golden lanyards scarred roll of flesh. Love my scars. Then she ceased surviving. I thought she was right. To die in youth, before charm's sun sets.

It's a question of war letters, he calls her Douce, Douce, or perhaps it's a *t*? Douce, Doute, Sweet, Doubt, he was so sad the other day, the Letter reports, and still more so to look sad and to leave you and to feel that you felt my sadness and that it would sadden you for me or that it would feel to you like distance or even an accusation, there was no such thing, there is no distance no accusation, there is a pursuit, I am hounded, that's all, by, by what in fact, by whom? Says his Letter. And at the same time I need that. I think only of **my death**. It's perhaps **my life**. I think I will not see you this week. Write to me. Tell me when we will see one another. And that nothing will ever change. Paris May 23 2:30 P.M. Says his Letter.

The letters are long. When she takes some out she no longer knows where she is. He is in a City. How many cities she has received. Dozens of explosions. Marseille. Vienna. Trieste. In the letter box.

How not to run after him, run him off? She runs after herself. She adores him. With what a trembling adoration she does not understand him. She tries not to understand him without making a mistake. But how not to make a mistake? She finds peace in his poems: I mean: her peace. It's because everything has a name in his poems in particular what has no name in life, all the rendings, all the plasterings, all the unbelievable mendings. In the poems the pains do not hurt her.

In the letters the joy she finds has a madwoman's face.

I buy Olivier de Serres with the golden lemons. We never talk about the concentration camp.

VII

FAITHFULLY FOREVER

Why did I keep the first letters, the letters before the letters, given that my nature is to throw things away, why did I keep the generic letter **Dear Madam thank you very much for your I would be very happy with you I am usually free on Wednesdays sincerely** I translate Madam I thank you for your letter I would be very happy to fix a meeting it would no doubt be best I am usually free on Wednesdays please accept Madam the signs of my respect, odorless letters at the time which today go up in incense. This miracle would almost make me believe in God. I didn't keep them, I don't keep, some force causes me to throw out, I have thrown out letters from people dear to me or at least these letters were thrown out without my being able to save them, I didn't wake up with a start, I didn't condemn or choose, I tore up very little in my life letters have disappeared that deserved life and the greatest care, I could cite some, there are letters I regret from Cortázar, letters from Genet, certain ones from Foucault, several from Derrida, I'm not boasting or accusing myself, I see no explanation, the affection between us was cloudless, if they are reading me or hearing me they know that there was no ill intention

there are likewise letters I regret from my children whom I love more than myself, no one will be able to doubt that,

I became aware of these. There is no word. Inexpropriations of myself – when I turned over my correspondence to the beautiful Bibliothèque Nationale de France I discovered that a large part of my treasures was missing. Since I had not kept them it cannot be said that I had lost them. They were no longer where I thought they were. I refuse any interpretation. Merely the facts: the only letters that resisted the shipwrecks, changes of address, *actes manqués*, are *all* of yours – from the first one – that could properly be called a "letter," a piece of circular mail, absolutely and for nothing. There was no intention. It was before the unconscious. I didn't keep them. I didn't throw them out. At least during our first years. Then I started to become a frenetic keeper.

What would I say about these letters?

First of all that they are not paper-letters, except in appearing to be so, they are your flesh and my blood.

And yet: I totally forgot them and you don't remember them at all.

They are behind us like our forebears and our gods.

They will be in front of us like our gondolas for crossing the dead.

They are with us like our commandments

They are not talkative, they are builders

Where were they living? In an old brown envelope that I had borrowed from something you sent. But I didn't remember it. When I looked for them, a few days ago, I didn't know their exact address or in which drawer, in which container they had been gathered together at the time of a general overturning of the household a few years before, whether it was a box, a file, a shipping pouch, a thick or ordinary envelope, it seemed to me that discretion had urged me then toward a plain material, but there were several brown envelopes in my drawers, I didn't find in the first, or in the second, on the third vain attempt I was suddenly flooded with an acute terror. I had to shift everything because I had not, as far as I knew, taken care to put them away beneath an immediately recognizable cover I had to take out all the notebooks from all the drawers, I had no idea of the size of the collection, I had never organized these letters. I had never gathered all your letters. I imagine that they are living in separate groups. Some of them moreover were slipped into notebooks, there was perhaps a dialogue between these little sheets, I never exercised authority over the movements of these souls. Now around my legs, I was kneeling in front of the meter-high drawers, there were dozens of notebooks, a swath of notepads, of envelopes all different in appearance, in size, fat ones, flat ones, boxes, I was taking out and I was shoving back in. The absence in the second drawer became: failure

The failure caught fire, no sooner had I touched the key of the third set of drawers than I was possessed by an idea of total catastrophe: if I don't find these letters I have killed, there will have been the greatest crime ever committed in the History of Love, I will not even have destroyed these letters,

I would not have – my chest heaving with restrained sobs – taken my car, without letting the obstacles that reality had piled in my madwoman's path stop me, without renouncing my maniacal plan I would not let myself be cooled down by the sudden difficulty of getting my car out of the parking lot, as if I no longer recognized the machine or the gears, I would not, after a quarter hour of grotesque maneuvers that depicted a dangerous state, have taken cognizance, wanted to take cognizance of the horror of the act I was going to commit no, I would have finally torn my car away from myself, and while lurching it down the streets without any hesitation, only some external obstacles, I will have gone without being able to tell how, all the way to the river, all the way to the bank, all the way to the quay, I could have been satisfied with the bridge, but nothing would satisfy me, I will have insisted on seeing the water face to face, in an unflinching frenzy I will have taken out of my briefcase all the trembling living meowing letters that I will have stuffed in there with a cruelty meant to be done with – but with whom with whom with whom? – and then there, with my briefcase on the ground sitting by my side I will, standing, pouring waves of tears, have taken your letters two by two, I will have torn them in four and if possible into smaller pieces, thus I will have killed and drowned them I will have willingly – although the will may not have been mine – put an end to these beings of goodness I will not even have drowned half my soul with your letters, all would have escaped my passion even the ultimate act, I will flutter from now on like a swerving bat, I will not even be able to say the word "letters" any more, letters? I will say, no, no letters, he never wrote, I will go on forever killing and dying I will repeat the crime, the shame, the pain and may time tear my bloody tongue from my mouth, I don't understand myself, will I then have attained without warning *a third lucidity*? I scratched, I rooted, I dug, I cast sideways glances the world by my side was becoming very small, the earth is leaving me no it's I who have left the earth, no I let the earth leave me, as if I were preceding myself into distress "I am punished to death" I thought.

I will thus not even have *acted* I thought – my chest heaving with sobs that suddenly welled up like an uncontrollable tide but that I crushed in my throat – while missing the keyhole, blind as I am without no less than within.

If I don't find these letters – it's not that I will never forgive myself, what use have I for forgiveness – I will be accountable before you and before me, separately, for monstrous and totally inexplicable crimes, I will be able to say absolutely nothing I will not be able to deny a hideousness that I can neither affirm nor recognize,

what would I say if while backing my car I had crushed one of my children? I think of that all the time

The word "infanticide," the word "monster" and the word "dying" are written large before me before the drawer

Not only, I thought – while checking the keys, perhaps I had the wrong key and risked breaking the key in the lock, an added misfortune – would I not have done it *on purpose*, I would not – it's not an excuse but all the same – have obeyed one of those urges of absolute terror that rise from the tomb of some archaic religion in which for centuries now no one any longer puts faith but whose evil emanations can still cloud the brain of an anxious passer by

I will not have even *attended* the massacre, it will not even have been a massacre, or drama, or spectacle, or act,

it's as if while backing the car I had said to myself: I hope the little ones are not crouching right there in the driveway and thereupon I step on the accelerator, and it's my own heart that I crush.

There is no reason. There is only some god. I believe and I don't believe. I believe in the absolute goodness that is a madness. I believe in the presence of evil that is anywhere at all one doesn't know why.

I opened the third drawer and the second envelope was it. Acquitted. I sat down first on the divan. I took twenty letters, those that were on top, the others I put back in the envelope no place in particular, in the drawer. I was in a hurry, I had to catch a plane.

I have come back to my mother's house. Why did I bring these letters? For days I seek the answer.

I am in the house in the South they are in the house in the North. All at once I take a plane, I go to get them. Otherwise I could no longer look at myself.

Slave, my mother says.

I am leaning over my desk. The letters are here now. At least a certain number of them.

Why have I brought back these and not those?

I don't dare argue. I might have brought back thirty of them?

As for the decision to go to the letters, it's this book that willed it. It happened so quickly.

Otherwise you will write no more.

– Your slave work, says my mother. She is standing behind my back bent over my desk. She isn't reading. She is observing.

– You let yourself be put in chains, says my mother

– By whom, I say

– Yes, says my mother.

By whom.

– I lean on you I say

– You are leaning on a bent reed.

In the plane I thought: I should have made photocopies. I wasn't able to. Why wasn't I able to make photocopies? In fair weather and good times I don't make photocopies. I was sitting by the aisle. I couldn't wait. The little boy in the window seat turns off the lights. Turn them on, I say. I cannot do anything other than take the letters out of the envelope, and be theirs. I read them quickly if that is called reading I read them at one blow at once one after the other I plunge the knife into my neck, they hurt me, I roll on my side I didn't expect this pain, "**Don't be mad at me**" he says, "I'm not mad at you" she says without taking her eyes off him, holding him in a gaze that flows, so much larger than any gaze, a gaze for all living gazes. The little boy in the window seat turns out the light.

And I forget. What has just happened. I try to retain the image
of what I've seen. I no longer move, I hope. It doesn't come
back. That's good. Thus the first reading in the plane had been
stolen, spirited away. A theft, a flight without duration. The
little boy is in on it, I say to myself.

They are small, lovely, with a fine-featured face, neat, the
words set down gracefully on the envelope, as if drawing a
portrait. I am in the house in the South with my mother, and
I am not reading them.

They are with me and I run from them. I write and I do not
live them, didn't see them. The cats however are on vacation.
They go down dig open books closets, archaeologize the folds
of the house, occupy the drawers, Aletheia and Philia, I read
them, I am the cats, but the letters that I flew off to get from
one plane to another, repose –

For eight days I want more that anything in the world to
bring them back to life but without managing to calm my
soul's recoil, a feeling that is too warped, inverted, compli-
cated for me to be able to reduce it to the name of jealousy.
One runs away from oneself when one flees, I was fleeing my
flight. And *in front of* the letters that were lying before me,
among my piles of paper, I will pass by without a caress, with-
out a thought, without a word.

Eight days later after the day in the plane, when I "do" my
"second" reading, overreading letter after letter from the salu-
tation to the signature, in an extremely quick non-stop fash-
ion, by reason of this speed I am spared the reception of one
feature, I subtract time. And I read from high above, I rely on
my age, my knowledge, my office, to the side, as if I were your
witness, the letter's and yours. From where I stand, I see you,
I see us you, through a spy-glass, I make out in the letters that
are so lovely and so small the serious and passionate faces that
we wore with that emotion I feel today when, from the dis-
tance of so many centuries brought close in the heart, reading

the description of feelings strong enough to promise life and death to creatures from the end of the German fourteenth century, I experience again exactly our own vertigos. Thus we will always have been the same ones as those two I say to myself. How I envy the one to whom you send these fears in New York. How I ache for her, an out-of-place feeling. How did we get to me from her? I can see that the decisions of fate were played out in the incredible force enveloped in these papers. But *before* this force, there must have been another authority, something like the odor of God in the bushes that attracted Moses inevitably toward the hidden word. Otherwise why would this letter have survived that will later become the first one, the only one of its kind, the invaluable one, signed **sincerely**.

The odor-of-God-in-the-bushes-before-the-fire-is-set will not have manifested its presence through the ordinary senses. It can only have been a mystical, non-human odor whose presence will have been proved by the effect on the subject called to the bush.

There was perhaps an olfactory suggestion of olive tree in the envelope with its neutral face. *Coups de théâtre* are not announced. Love my work, love the back of the checkbook on which I scribbled five words overheard in a café. I was moreover so far from any premonition that I myself wrote a division on the back of the third letter, I must have been doing my household accounts. Two letters later such graffiti will scar my brain if, not by my doing naturally, it came about on the body of one of the missives incarnated as beings who can be threatened by death, this taking on a fated effect as of 13.12.1965.

I see nothing special about the typical "letter" from 18.4.1964 sent on 20.4.1964, carefully dated, later you add the hour at which your hand touches the paper of my cheek, I should have thrown out this unaddressed mail that would subsequently assume the rank of letter, and an exceptional place since it is the non-letter among the letters, it was written to Idon'tknowwhoitdoesn'tmatter, as for me I had read you I knew to whom, to which poem in truth, I must have written to you in your language and you answered me in the most English English the least poetic the most impeccable the least subjective the most respectful that is to say the most courteous the most blind the most perfectly insignificant, and I didn't throw out this missive, I didn't lose this bulletin, the non-letter is now the source of the Ganges, there is not one sign of the flood and of the future immensity the thing is composed according to the policed rules, its commas carefully placed, it is methodically amiable, neither bourgeois nor aristocratic, neither burning nor icy and I didn't throw it out neither colloquial nor cavalier nor marking frontiers. All is mystery. When I *saw* this non-letter from before Everything in the airplane for the first time looked at it and saw – for I certainly had not *looked at* this mailing, I must have noted and followed the indications – I was enchanted. That we had come from this little nothing! It was already the envelope of what would follow, but then it was a characterless envelope, the paper too was nothing special, it was already yours but I knew that only later. So, what? A finish, a precision, a precise imprecision, detailed brought to term free on Wednesday between 10:00 and 12:00 and in the afternoon, Thursday between 2:00 and 4:30, Saturday afternoon. You would need only to write to me a week before you come by, a precision in the imprecision. A fine elevated writing set to the rhythm of dreamed-of capital letters, as if the whole poem had taken refuge in the forms of hand-written letters. Non-letter without face without gaze but not without body.

I didn't look at it, I'm convinced of that.

Everything is number, each number is an individual, this letter was an individual, I didn't know it, someone sensed it. The universe speaks I thought, except that its language is incomprehensible, I looked at this "letter" in the plane. Dreaming about all that this letter-being already knew, before anything, any event, about you, about what could happen and not happen. Finally I thought there was something extraordinary in this letter: it was the non-poem *par excellence*. At that moment the little boy in the window seat turned out the light.

The third reading took place on Tuesday, July 27. I had made up my mind. This time I had a rendezvous at myself, I am always on time. The time: 9:30. I was there. I was on your side: I see you writing. You are pressed for time, your flanks jostled by wars, you hasten to slip these little leaves between the jaws of time. From the height at which you are writing on your knee, between the doors that are constantly opening, the utterances have the suddenness of lightning. You have to say the essential thing in two lines. Moreover grave matters are brief. Here where you are – it's the war – on your side. Shots are being fired from all directions. Billows of white smoke rise into your sky. There where I am – I didn't know. From where you are you cry out to me that one mustn't forget **my mortal frailty**. I hadn't even thought about it, I recognize clearly in this my myopia, my ignorance. I never think of the mortal's frailty. I'm ashamed of my insouciance. I can thus see that you have to tell me everything. You bring yourself toward me in the tumult, you are going to tell me *a* word – you say to me, the word for moving from my ordered world stacked with books to your universe swept with thoughts – this word you tell me is the

which word were you going to say? was it a name? a key? – in the place of whom or of which a famous captain of war has just situated himself – you see you tell me I have just now overcome him. I am the victor in this swordfight, but he took up my time, he cut the lines – "and it is the pieces, the shreds of present life" that remain, that you send me, pieces of

– I'm up to the soldier's seventh letter. I'm exhausted

One by one I received them in the past. Between two let-
ters existence. My second lucidity. I wrote my thesis with
repugnance out of love. I traveled. Certain letters caught up
with me. London says the envelope, New York, Yale. Did I
read them? The letter from Hue? I mean did I read them with
my eyes open? Was I facing them? Or sidewise? Was I sitting
beside the hero? The scene can be played in many different
ways. He can be standing, seated, turned toward me, never
look at me, read out his texts in front of him, head lowered,
cast them far away from himself, toward a horizon to be imag-
ined. I could be on the edge of the scene. I could prefer to keep
to the side. To listen to him, bowed down, as he speaks over
me, to stand behind him, my hand close to his shoulder with-
out ever touching him, to follow the rush of his gaze as if I
could see over there what he already sees, what he announces
to me and describes to me and that I don't see here. But
between two bursts of fire, I had the time to withdraw into my
libraries, I forgot perhaps the sequence, perhaps I called these
first blazing drafts letters, I must have believed that they were
written even, or wanted to believe it, at that time I did believe
that poems were literary objects, the hiccups of pain that pro-
duced rejections, extinctions of syllables, precipitations, I
found this so beautiful, I was enthused, I kept the idea of
sorrow at a distance from my jubilation, still today I read you
while forgetting you, I enjoy your poems in a state of
impudent detachment, to know for which hell they are com-
pensation is only knowledge, the joy of beauty remains apart
from torments, I go from our pain to the act of grace in a
minute (all the same it has to be a long minute). But today
seven letters without interval dissipate the peace, defenses
aren't put in place, I force myself to receive the eighth letter
and when I read the so very French *"fidèlement pour toujours,"*
"faithfully forever," as if I were receiving for the first time the
violent thrust of your palm against my chest I cannot pretend

that I didn't hear what I didn't hear no doubt then when they raised their scraps of fire from time to time toward my face. I am exhausted. I am sad and I am delighted to have been the one that in the past received without receiving, and yet received the order to keep my eyes closed.

Blitz campaigns, and I didn't know that it was war. History comes later, it's at war with itself. The war of 64–73. How they attacked. How they resisted. How they took power right away in the first year. Our power. They conducted battles. Against whom? They are so strong. They are forces. They couldn't not decide, I say to myself, whether this or that, and even perhaps everything. How were you able to write the word "faithfully" four times after having written it the first time right after the letter of more-afraid-than-ever dated 13.12.65 in which you declared to me your "reservations," "withdrawals," "selfish precautions," "disturbance of being," how were you able to write it the first time, the fourth time and then later take the disturbance of being as far as "faithfully forever," I wonder, and later you sign several letters "faithfully," perhaps the *faithfully* after the *faithfully-forever* is another faithfully? – an other faithfully? Had it become a faithfully of letters? Perhaps the one before the faithfully-forever was more timid, more anxious quivering held back feigning restrained warmth, perhaps it felt a little too much and not enough, perhaps it felt by dint of repeating itself a fever rising, a dizziness, that would precipitate it, make it insist all the way to excess, to that commitment *forever* or in other words that disturbance-forever but how then to explain *afterwards* the faithfullys that follow, are they less are they more, are they the last rumblings of the bush that cannot extinguish the outburst of its voice with a single stifling? Are they these faithfullys the last shudders of a madman's howls? Or the withdrawal, the lull after the convulsion, the detumescence of a word, the death rattle of a god's dream of faithfulness? Or else nothing. But *nothing* without any meaning is impossible it seems to me for the master of poems.

– I don't remember, you say.

– *Fidèlement* is a beautiful word, you say, greedy for words as you are

– *Fidèle ment* I say, *faithful lies.* An expression that wouldn't exist today. Who would write that today?

– Who wrote it? I say.

The being who you are cannot say that, I say. But these letters were from the disordered-being.

– But is fidelity an ordering? Is it not disorder, disturbance itself, but hidden, crooked, straightened out?

– Fidelity, I say, how the word defies. It's the word that denounces the infidel I say, but, at the time, I don't think I thought that. But the ardent reader that I was thought it perhaps. I who lived for reading, I who was making my first distressing literary discoveries, I who was beginning to see fidelity infidelize itself as soon as it touched on Joyce, Kafka, Milton, I who was beginning to see – and that to swear literature is to have to betray

And what to think of the letter of 20.1.1966, also a faithfully – a letter of a lacerated beauty, so beautiful, so lacerated, that it seems to have been torn alive out of one of the poem collections (I'm thinking of **The Truth Truly** of course) but that's not the case – your letters have never been former or future poems – the letter that I will call from now on the *letter-to-the-limit* – when I want to refer to it – a letter that traces on the earth the ultrafine edging, the lifeline without thickness on which you see us maintaining the life of our life – what to think of such a letter when I notice upon examining the envelope: (1) that it bears an extraordinary predestinal postmark that I did not see before. It has two squares in which are lodged on the left a telephone dial with the number 16 at its center. The circles of the dial are blank, as in my nightmares.

The dial has blank eyes. On the right it's a clock's dial that looks at me, the hours are indicated by slender lines the hands are fat and set on eight o'clock. These two figures are exactly the little monsters that come back in hundreds of dreams, I spend lifetimes conjuring these two planets polishing them waxing them with glances, I have ruined my eyes on these round eyes, it's the first time I see the two eyes of my life's demon staring at me together. These two circles are inserted in a toppled H: ⊐⊏, it's my letter aghast, that says at the top: "long-distance calls using 16," at the bottom: "cheaper after 8 P.M.," and on the median bar between the two eyes: "and easier." The mark on the stamp says: "Paris XIII 1 H Av. de Choisy – 13."

I am pointed out, followed, recognized, condemned, who could doubt it, people are trying to hypnotize me.

And thereupon: (2) that you addressed this letter to yourself, to *my* name at *your* summer address, at your mother's. How did this letter ever reach "my house"? *Your* address is crossed out. The time-eyes of the Post Office were supervising. I was then in the house in the South at postal code 33. I owe a life – I owe this letter and this oath of fidelity to the unknown man or woman at the Post Office, some official in charge of correspondence dramas. The overseer of calls using 16.

Inside this letter it's a question of living-all-the-same. And what if it had never arrived?

Did it ever arrive? To whom? Who was I? Who have I been, who have I ceased to be? And you, who are you, and no longer remember. Did-it-arrive-all-the-same? A letter addressed to me-at-your-house at your mother's house? Or to non-me *à jamais chez toi*, for(n)ever at your home? And what does "*à jamais chez toi*" mean in this context of "joyful pain"?

In this letter it was a question of *véritée*, of a somewhat old-fashioned, or superseded *véritée*, of supertruth, with its shadowy part that ends it and limits it, you were saying, and I surely asked myself, if I know me, with terror, surely, what is a *vérité limitée*, a limited truth, and whether I was and where I was *véritée*, and you *le vérité*, or whether I was, thrown, on the other side or whether it was an error.[6] All of these questions must have tortured me. I know myself: I see everything. I see that I don't see. I don't see that I don't see. I see you and I don't understand you, is that seeing? I received these letters drop by drop and I tasted the violence at leisure. Or else

Then I put myself in doubt

Then I forget.

One can't receive such letters without doubting myself.

And to think that you signed faithfully, as if you were making a sign of the cross with a knife, on the chest, mine or yours.

But this letter should not have arrived to me. What was your intention?

– I don't remember at all, you say.

I was reading the letter that almost failed to arrive, and a gloom fell over me: to whom was this letter faithful, or unfaithful, by arriving at-my-home-all-the-same? There are thus fidelities that are faithful forever and fidelities that are not forever? And me reading and becoming gloomy was I not unfaithful? I didn't even know to whom to attribute or to whom to receive this letter. Or *to whom* I was faithful, if it was to you or to the venerated poet? To your name adored before you. If it wasn't me, if it wasn't you, all these faithfullys on one side and the other and this faithfully forever could have been merely inadvertent, amorous awkwardness, or Octave's getting carried away with Armance –

---

[6] This passage changes the standard grammar and gender of *la vérité*, truth. When it's written with a final mute e, *véritée* is turned into an adjective with a feminine subject. But it is also doted at one point with a non-standard masculine article, *le vérité*, when the subject is masculine. (Tr)

but near you the words speak, each one with each other one and all the others confer with each other, swearing and clashing together.

I cast glances at the letters, I go from fright to delight – Awful letters, I tell you. I don't know if you knew – I remember nothing at all. I'd like you to show me one of them some day. I remember the tone. I wrote in English?

– In French, I say.

One I say is impossible. It's a matter of an army. A cavalry. Was it a rout? Was it a triumph?

I don't know how to read them faithfully today. I read as if. A difficult trick of the heart to work out.

– A letter that says fidelity while envisioning its opposite in a foreign language I was saying to myself, what does it say to me in truth? In truth all the same?

– Run. Run it says.

But Kafka always signed: *Dein*, he clung to Milena, he said to her: hold me, hold your yours, but what are you waiting for, what are you doing? Don't read my letter it exists merely to lead one to a single word. To the letter signed: *Nein*. No one will ever know if the *Nein*-letter had been signed *Nein*, no, in good conscience or by some forking of the tongue.

As soon as I read "faithfully forever" my head grew cold, my heart iced over, I put on a sweater I added a jacket, one can't dispel a chill within. It was so much a promise, I feared immediately, a promise is stronger than anything. I'm afraid I won't see the limit of light.

For days I try to read the letters; after several days I realize that they are escaping me, they are hiding under files, among books, in baskets of mail I spend more time looking for them than leafing through them, I find the mother-envelope half empty, at the end of the week I think that I will never have read them. I count them, it's my sacred flock. I will never know how many I brought with me, I find nineteen of them in the morning and twenty-one in the evening it leaves me no peace. This then is the "pursuit of happiness" I say to myself, this terrifying sensation that *one* of them is always *missing*, one less or one more. All of them or almost all make way for God's paw. It's not I but you who open the door for him, which altogether astonishes me. At the instant I am noting this as it comes to mind, they are sleeping, all together, at least I think so. Snuggled up together. I would do better not to touch them anymore, but I hear a call and what a call! It must have been ringing out for a long time and very loud without managing to overcome my deafness, to burst out so loud and all at once. My god! And I open the envelope again and they pour out and they fill my eyes like tears come from you. I look for god or God. He is hiding. I see clearly that he is the hidden principle of hiding, the hidden king of letters, that's how he manifests himself: by hiding himself, with atheisms. Because he is the marvelous thing in which you do not believe and who does not need you to believe in order to be. And the lesson to be drawn is that you too, my god, you might be, without my having either to believe or not in the word forever, to which all the same I am indebted for my having loved you before I ever met you.

God – in which I do not believe but God has no use for your evasions, he's hidden beneath a pile of papers in the corner of the cage – God-in-which-you-don't-believe is his name, is this enormous pile of reticulated rings, at first glance they look like sections of tires, he doesn't move his coil clinging to the bars of the cage ends in a fine lovely head with an uninterpretable smile, his unmoving eyes sparkle eternally on the lookout, God is in the cage, he looks at us he looks at the Lion, he stares at Philia our Lion, this God doesn't bite, he doesn't exist, he is himself the cage in which our Lion dreams he has entered like love enters into horror,

God that you don't renounce moves about between the leaves of the seventh letter. He extends a magnificent golden paw between the atheisms, after all you are calling him in reverse, and by force of denying him and of praying him, and of pray-denying him and teasing him, you will have ended by provoking him and invoking him, and by the eighth letter he is there. He is there in us around us foreveround us like the bars to which we cling like the pillars of the temple that encloses us on 5.3.65. And you turn us over to him, in which you don't believe.

– We cannot see each other on Thursday you say "early morning foggy and despairing," says the letter to quote you. I imagine today the fog and the despair of yesterday, but who despairs, I wondered in March 65, and already with the first words my heart clouds up like a sky, and the early morning, who's that? I wondered, and I surely said to myself what have I to do with the early morning, my love is stronger than the fog, and thereupon the sentences lost their subject pronoun in this all-too-real fog. "Am early" said one. "Went to bed at 2 A.M." ("Celan was dining at the house") "Got up at 7 A.M." said the letter. You can see that there is reason to despair after a seven-hour parenthesis with Celan only a poem in a parenthesis, but that could explain the fog, the early morning, the disappearance of the subjects, the desperately that is gaining ground, poetry is killing him, that's his paradox, Proust's paradox, Celan's, the paradox of his dead or dying friends killed by the approach of poetry, life itself is killing them, you understand? I understand, yes, yes I think that I must understand. I had warned you says the letter. Very Very Little Presence: Much Poetry and not too much Presence. Otherwise I will not be able to see us the letter was saying. Did I read it? Did I see it? I looked at it I'm convinced of that. It is so beautiful, so wonderfully drawn, the fine, hurried lines, a wind blowing from the right side of the letter. And the punctuation marks, everywhere ellipses, quiverings, dashes, brackets; and the parentheses. As if you were pushing the bed aside, discovering a trap door that, once the secret stairs are descended, opens onto the forest. There waiting for you for hours is a doe or a dog, a bitch, a faithful one, ready to be pursued when you like. There where the beast devoured by impatience and patience joined together, motionless around its heart contemplates the forest still empty of her master. Did I read or did I see the paragraph "I think of you who know [almost] all the 'centers' of my life. Perhaps you have a better idea what its center can be?" to which you had added the word *unique*. *Unique* center. Did I see or did I read the face of true distraction? What did I think on reading and receiving these handfuls of sparks followed by the poem **"A short note, I tell you."** This note to tell you above all, the letter said, that I will not be free Thursday, don't worry, I believe in our light, but Thursday no, Fridayno

Can we *see one another* Tuesday, you say in the terrible letter written at the colorless dawn at the barrier to Hell, not Friday or Saturday Sunday impossible Monday no Tuesday *see one another if you agree* you say, **forgive me** my silences my haste my *actes manqués*, my slips **forgive me** Thursday I say every day **forgive me** if not Tuesday *see one another if*, tell me that you agree Tuesday, you who know [almost],

it seems to me that it is in this letter or in the other that you open the cage for us and we enter into god like the Lion goes into the dream, beautiful himself as a god and trembling all over, and you say – but who are you then? – God. You say god and you close the door. You recite God-who-doesn't-exist a poem that from sublime becomes fearsome while going from the paper to the burning cage, you invoke God *in reality* the better to attract him, defy him, require him, God as witness and servant, as tamed tamer of the Lion's love. "God in French, you recite, *that* very thing which should be so as to *see us/see one another* and repair our death at every instant," I listen to you and I don't listen to you I lick your paw, I slip my tongue between your words, I groom your breast, our death at every instant you say, God should be, it would be necessary that he be, he is the idea of what should make for *that, see us/see one another*, if not Monday then Tuesday,

he should be, it ought to be,

he exists as such, like this thought in us

with his nine meters of reticulated rings coiled in the right corner of our cage

he thus exists, you recite, as, in us, the life of our death.

The letter ends with death. The last line is composed: "of our death." You send me three letters that end with our death.

Then you slide the volume of *Letters from Artaud* to Genica Athanasiou into my letter box.

– I don't remember that, you say. Why did I do that I am going to reread these letters, you say.

I was so afraid of "God" at Olivier de Serres, I was so afraid of That-which-should-be, and terrorized of your fear, I entered the Olivier de Serres cage hoping and fearing, hoping and fearing. The houses across the way are on fire. They are destined for destruction. What worries me are the bits of soot. I'm afraid they will reach your car. As for the rest, the world can burn.

It was the day of *Letters from Artaud* in the Box. You must help me you wrote, and you underlined twice you must help me, once by writing these words in very large letters, twice by drawing a very large line, my life is so fragile, the life of my life is too uncertain. *You must help me*, screamed the letter, *but in which sense?* it screamed. PLEH!

But in which sense? From which side? I was panicked. I ran left and right. I want to give you drink, and I don't know if it's too much or too little

I was reading Celan, Artaud, all those foggy and despairing early mornings that prowled their phantoms in the forest, I was living very close to those near me who were so familiar, I was afraid of catching their misery and their illness of being crushed by being. How could I have run to your aid if I fell under the weight of your charm? NALEC!

According to the letters, the love between Artaud and Genica lived in France from 1921 until December 25, 1940 –
lived, was killed, and revived
And during all this time – was living
Lived.
Beginning in January 1941 Genica changed into *heroin(e)*
The letters changed into magic arrived without postmark, letters in powder.
Pain is a quality of truth in flesh and bone –
It's a solitude, love itself
It's a betrayal that is not committed voluntarily.
– Why did I give you the Letters said to be from Artaud? For a thousand reasons that I can't talk to you about here for a thousand reasons.
It's a matter of allusions of metaphors and of innuendos
It's a matter of intentions and insinuations that are all excellent
I guess as to the moods but I do not say them
– Was it a warning?
If it was a self-portrait, then whose?
Why didn't you give them to me instead of leaving them in the letter box of the building as if it were a Letter, as if you didn't want to sign this letter of letters with your hand but with another's
Or else as if you were telling me not to want to be the being who writes such letters
Or who could become the being –
What did you want, to do, to avoid, with them, with me?

And I received them.

– Or a threat?

– But a book left in a box and not given is a letter from phantom to phantom

– I have forgotten

– No one will ever know who will have written these letters to whom?

The Absence-of-Telephone has occult powers. They cannot be controlled. Without the Absence-of-Telephone would you have ever written me the letter of June 17, 1966, which will later become The Letter of Fate? Initially the Hole of Fate has no dimension. It goes unnoticed. A needle hole in the hull of a ship. The letter bearing the seal of the Post Office says the seal of Defense. The envelope speaks: *Civil/ Defense/ A Necessity/ A Duty*, and nobody listens to it. The whole letter inside and out seems to have been struck by the necessarily bad fate that you were talking to me about at length within

In the plane I look at it once, I knock on wood. So I say to myself, *she*, this letter, is there. That is the face *she* wore. So there exist fated spells that have not even been cast voluntarily by the sender. It is *Fate* in person who has been busy. Otherwise who could have mobilized public services, the Post Office, the Railways, and all the private interests of the various subjects in order to pull off such a feat? A sly, treacherous, lightning performativity sleeps with one eye open. An apparently innocent but inoculating letter, with a little bit of evil eye spread over the paper as are scattered throughout a destiny the seeds of tragedy, a powder, an infinitesimal powdering, a little of not-very-much in the words, in the question marks. Like a letter from the seventeenth century, one of those letters that are pain machines in analytic novels (letters of the fatal orange tree, letters in *The Princess of Clèves*, letters from the Duchesse de Langeais, etc.) all those letters that kill themselves trying to protect the love of life. Or of death? A necessity. A duty. A dual seeing: a necessity.

Was the June 17, 1966, letter with its motto "Psychic defense a necessity a duty" obeying its postal law, or was it contravening, when it went running left and right following my footsteps, missing me at every address, arriving at the central Post Office in Bordeaux on June 15 when I had just left the city so as to miss me on June 16 in Paris which I had just left again in the direction of the Southwest chasm my soul besieged by definitive sorrow and renunciation, without any sign from you having come to calm the terror, fed entirely by weakness and the consent that served me as a substitute for you, I remember my falling apart, my specter in the train, its bent head not protesting the severity of the gods, its broken posture on the second-class seat, where I saw myself deported toward the familiar Hell, where I withdrew on June 17 into the mental convent set aside for victims of those attacks classically attributed to a purely technical misfortune: problems with the mail, with clocks, with the messenger, mistaken addresses, wrong phone numbers. And finally stamped and scarred all over it arrives, the letter, sent back from Paris to the Southwest. How feverishly it takes up the defense of you, of me, of faith?

"Let me try to explain to you the causal chain of events that happened," it would have said to me on the Thursday that followed the events that happened on Tuesday if it had reached me then. But finally after the event, nothing kept me in Paris any longer, I had left on Thursday, after the Tuesday Absence had broken out, followed by the world's long silence. Immediately it takes the train again for the Post Office in Bordeaux which, social, professional familial time having gone by as always, I leave so as to return with horror to this Paris where now reigns over the squares, in the streets, Your indisputable Absence.

Freud? No. At the time I had not read Freud. But that would not have changed anything. Putting names to pains and fears does not sew up the wound. "You ought, no you ought not, to toss me back on the pile of all-those-who and who you were telling me about last week" you ought and you ought not, you recognize there the language that appalls you, those are two different yououghts, said my bush, that's what you always say about language, the fact that language always plays these double tricks on us, you know what I wanted to say to you,

Psychic defense, a duty

"Let me try to explain to you the *causal chain of events.*" When I looked at the letter, the second time, while anchored to my desk, escorted by trees and years, thirty-eight years having gone by with their events and causal chains, I contemplated it with the uneasy admiration of the age-old curiosity of Marlowe seeking in the face of Helen of Troy the summary of the thousand ships launched onto the rocks of nothingness, with the serious distress of Pascal bent in thought over the idea of Cleopatra's nose. Such a little thing, the curve of an eyebrow, a cheekbone, the end of a nose: the face of the earth: the sex of hell. A letter. I move its entire earth and its armies, its princes, its feelings. What a *je-ne-sais-quoi!* Where is the *quoi*, the *quoi* of the nose that will would have, has, I don't know and never will know, changed the whole known universe under the name of Olivier de Serres? The body marvelously harmonious, a well-balanced letter, in all senses of the word.

It dashes on and instantly it can be seen piling up "the events" that "came about in a period of incredible agitation in which I can no longer locate myself" you say, and which I cannot talk about here. Instead one must imagine heaps of mountains that entail gaps of time and space, encounters with giants of thought, among which a dinner for Friday evening with the most elusive, the most delicate, the most touchy the most furtive, Wednesday evening I realize that Friday is impossible. But Celan is leaving for Berlin from there the lunch that finally will assume the unpredictable aspect that you know, at 6:45 *he was not moving yet* (you underline) *I didn't dare – for a thousand reasons* (I underline) – to rush him or, to say, that I had, *put yourself in my state of mind*, a rendezvous, and where, at 4:00. At any moment I thought he would leave, he wouldn't leave, I accompany him, I arrive at Olivier de Serres I thought at any moment, mental suffering is nothing, 6:45, but the *state of mind* in which I find myself not knowing where I am, *you imagine* in what state of mind I was. I am now all the way on top of a mountain of mountains, believe me, I can hear Pelion, Ossa cracking. The events are crushing me and also time. It was 7:45. You've been waiting for me for two hours.

For five hours multiplied by every thought of Obscurity, which are not thoughts but faceless horrors, I have not been waiting for you, I wanted to get up, stuff myself in the sleeve of Oblivion, lick my fur and my wounds, but I was not moving yet, for lack of strength, light, explanation, for lack of experience for lack of imagination and intelligence, for lack of greatness and divinity, later for lack of a letter and for lack of a telephone one loses one's reason, there is certainly another reason, what dreadful night of the spirit prevents my finding it.

You ought but no you ought not

How not to push away the idea of pushing you away

How to push away the idea

Put yourself in my state of mind. If you saw the state of Olivier de Serres. A swath of giants among which I am startled to see a poor monster a cat who appears to have two heads, a head in place of its tail, a kind of double cat, but while it crawls toward me, the swollen gaping belly horrifies me, the beast then opens its immense fish mouth and lets out a long cry, it is suffering atrociously, how suffering makes us into strangers, I didn't recognize my own suffering, one must make it stop immediately I say to myself I beg you, kill it! I say to myself. But how? I see myself taking a pot of water in my panic. Was I thinking of drowning it? Be patient for a second, we're going to find you a remedy. I see myself pouring the water on the head of the poor beast that is my head. I had so much pity that despite the enormous disgust that the open flesh provokes in me, I manage to force myself to pass my hand under the head-mouth, I caress, I find fur, I think that I am calming it, water is running down my face, then the suffering lets out once again an immense cry, now I have only one thought: kill it because it is as cruel as death but much more hideous.

The day after the double cat the letter of June 17 sweeps away the horrors of Olivier de Serres. How sweet life is after resurrection.

– **Will you forgive me?** You must, no you must not. You mustn't be angry with me sweet lamb I was with Desnos until 1:00 and he insisted at all costs on coming along and accompanying me home, I didn't dare tell him I didn't think I could tell him for a thousand reasons that my house *was your house that evening*. I told you many times that we would have trouble meeting and being *in flesh and in bone* present one to the other. You see?

I call you very quickly. I wait to have a little money so as to telephone you. I realize how insane the life we are leading is. Trust me. Who else? Nanaqui?

Letters? No. Executions of beasts so that God-the-one-who-should might pardon, if he exists, the excesses of happiness, the stolen moments of grace, the incredible impertinence of daring to howl with joy above the blazing fires and even if you order me "don't cry out! People will hear us," when I am the beast receiving your blows, I cry out and it's from joy. "Kill me!" I cried. "**Hold your tongue!** Don't cry out!" How difficult it is for you to form these words above my face, with your beautiful lips tensed to prevent your own cry from crying as well. Short, hard books, grievances, advances, the sayings of the other side,

Life has two faces one of shameless happiness the other of shameless pain.

VIII

WHEN I BECOME A FRENETIC KEEPER

at the beginning I am furtive, I hide without touching, because I want to hide from myself that I am keeping things that one doesn't keep in normal circumstances – it's not a question of things meant to be kept or thrown away like letters it's not a question of speaking things that have a little bit of spirit and a little bit mortality in them and commonly enjoy an unthinking respect – at the beginning I keep large padded envelopes in which books had arrived, on which your hand has written my address. My mother keeps large envelopes but not for long. At the first opportunity she reuses them. I keep the large envelopes secretly and in secret because it's forever. Even to myself I don't admit it. I slip them among thick piles of different papers. Without address and without destination. I don't have a crate for envelopes, no drawers. So what do I do? I send them. Where? Where. When. To go around the world that is made of time. It sometimes happens that one of them arrives at me. The journeys in the shelves can last for dozens of years. One has no news. One has no recollection. One day

I move a bunch of folders, and – like the deep-sea diver who finds in a sleeping galley an amphora sealed at its neck with wax and containing an oil, the same oil for three thousand years, the oil of three thousand years, and this amphora was worth the price of two slaves – I find a large white envelope perfectly preserved on which my name still feels the caress of your hand. It is worth two slaves. One must try to imagine the diver's emotion upon holding in his arms the unchanged living body whose haunches, thighs neck are still just as beautiful who bears in her round belly two slaves three millennia the dreams of a Greek merchant and his household all of Europe with the sea, the only thing this divinity lacks is arms and he's the one who provides them, now they form but one, and at that moment the life of the external body and the internal lives preserved outside of nothingness under death unite and produce in the diver's whole being such a discharge of the supernatural that he ejaculates on the amphora and it's as if he swears never to harm it. So he replaces it in the depths where she remains queen with a cortege of fish.

I kiss the forehead of the envelope, I kiss its eyelids. It is twenty years old, it is young. I put it back in the sea. Last year I found one that bore the stamp 1969. They enliven my places with their invisible navigations. This Sunday, August 8, 2004, my mother's life is rising again, she transfigures the garden path. Amphora of a century.

Living envelope.

You telephone. Our two witnesses come running. The cats prophesy what is and what will be. God gave us the cats who live more keenly and die more quickly than we do for witnesses.

We are learning to live with death, with the dead, we are learning with the life of our death in us, to live with cats with mother, with envelopes, with secrets, to live each instant, we are learning to live, we are learning but we don't know.

Envelopes of instants: are they life, are they death? The answer depends on my force of relife. Today I have the Force. Everything is living. Tomorrow, we'll see. Today I have the Force of ascent.

I am learning to live by heart.

"I am learning to live by heart": I say this sentence to you on the telephone. You hear: "I am learning to live by fear." That's us: heart and fear, *coeur* and *peur*, masculine and feminine. Aletheia and Philia the (feminine) *chattes* that I call (masculine) *chats*. Our olives and our torches: the latter can start a fire the former can catch it.

I don't know when or why I began keeping the large envelopes, plain or padded, white, brown. It may be that in the past I threw some out, I don't remember. Later on it became impossible for me to throw away an envelope from you. This impossibility of throwing-away spread, without calculation, without programming little by little, to all sorts of objects and substances. Once I non-threw-away a square of gauze with a drop of blood in the middle on one side and a piece of sticking plaster on the other side. You had come from a blood test. It seemed to me impossible to throw out this trace. That was some twenty years ago.

The storage of traces is something else. Everything that is paper returns to the paper that occupies an immense space in my dwellings. The mixture of sacred and non-sacred paper of all kinds happens naturally. The result is that a little bit of the sacred is propagated no doubt to the reams of printer paper as well as to all the ordinary and extraordinary paper stuffs that abound around me. I don't know when I began keeping traces of your sperm. In my view it must have been rather later in our history. I would date the *regular* keeping of your sperm to my last house-move. But it seems to me that I had begun for sure twenty years ago and perhaps more. I can't find in my memory the trace of a first event. If I had the patience and courage to reread my notebooks from the first twenty years, I would probably find a date, because I always noted everything. But I don't have the strength or the time to do this research above all I don't have the mental strength to go back up the stream of our turmoils. Happiness as well as unhappiness would make life as well as death more difficult for me. I imagine that what drove me to gather your sperm is a kind of jealousy between precious liquors, ink and sperm, for if ink is a sperm that wants to be kept, why should sperm that writes nobly always except when it's a question of voluntary procreation be treated as a substance whose value plummets after use? I see us on the witnesses' bed, one day when we had just nimbly rolled out the dough of the body, spread it out, reshaped it, remade it into a stronger more fertile whole, having satisfied that pain that *knows*, that calls for consolation, that mute call asking to be served a unique *dish* I see myself watching you tasting now the taste of repose. Not only the sculptured face. But first of all the head, the weight of the head, the rock, the posed head, the repose of rock the dense weight of repose. Head beneath its wing, my head your wing, hand on the belly in the dreaming position of two voyagers in time's ferry, the one carrying the other. We are talking. It was about: scheduling, the use of time. How time uses us. And about: notebook of texts. And about: cheese tart. We were floating in that air that neither wakes nor sleeps. Your liquor: slow foam at my belly. My lips at the silk of your underarm. I drink your dreams. My hand takes a Kleenex. The box on the bedside table. Wipes the Kleenex over the honey sperm. Otherwise a little puddle on the bedspread, a child's drawing, minimal pond. Could betray us. You having left, wash. As if it were a sin. No. Grace. Hidden grace. Grace's duty: to hide. Kleenex. In the past there wasn't any. The time without

Kleenex, without answering machine. Today love is better armed. In the past: wash, erase, destroy. Adieu! No! Stay! As if stillborn? Cadaver? No! Life! Stay! Kleenex. Marriage veil. Veils soaked with wedding nights, letters of eternities. Quietly, in the bedside table drawer. There too some of your hair. Black locks ash-colored locks and now dried honeys. My mother's voice: *du bist doch verrückt!* Imaginary voice. No one will ever know. Do not die! Stay, unreadable writing! But what is the date of this scene that returns to me with such force? And perhaps it is a scene after editing of scenes. For I see clearly the two witnesses stretched out at the southwest and the southeast of our earth-bed, to the left Aletheia, to the right Philia, between them: us. The two witnesses are not as old as the ritual. In the past we had only one witness, but I can't talk about that here. What did I do in the past? The annulling of the sperm is so inconceivable to me that I am in the state of sincere falsification. I claim that I never chased away, dismissed, cleaned up. Starting with that day bathed in gold which I do (not) recall exactly, I enter into a complicated devotion. Because Kleenex is not a sheet of paper. It cannot be slipped in or filed. It doesn't have the non-thickness of a letter. No matter. There is neither law nor example, after all. Nor do I have to worry about the space taken up by the bags. I am not devoid of good sense. If the house were to burn, a scenario that the frequency of fires in the region forces me to think about, it is the letters and the notebooks that I am ready to save, if circumstances permit it. As I see it the Kleenex treasure would meet a natural and magnificent end in the case of accidental fire. For my idea is not to constitute a library of spermed Kleenex. What I want is not to throw them out, not to treat what is noble, which is like the body's thought, like some snot.

Each time I cut a lock of your hair, I am obeying the whispers of metonymy. Whatever you have touched is you. I don't carry this gathering to the point of delirium. I do what I can. The paper napkins on which you will have wiped your lips at lunch, I keep them but within reason. I wipe my lips with the trace of your lips for a day or two, then I let the object go. Always. I keep the trace a little. It depends. If there are rules or decisions, I don't know what they are. There is no hesitation. No one will ever see me, holding some thing in my hands, squeezing myself. Things are decided and this so simply that I have only to follow a movement. Tickets (cinema, theater, subway – Paris, New York one time Tokyo, British Museum; antique tickets museum of antiquities Berlin-Dahlem July 1968, how beautiful and neurotic we were then), I keep obviously.

All those that I have not lost. When we were loaded like pistols, frightening, at the end of the sixties, bitten, myself losing myself I lost as well as I kept, not methodically, not consciously, as I could have lost my life without thinking in the seventies, there was too much power and too much powerlessness in front of the door, in the bedroom, in the hallway, time and its dust have changed them into pearls, could I imagine it one day, I thought I was losing you and losing me, not losing you but that you would lose me, and of our chapter on earth there would remain a paltry tomb of tickets, there's the summed-up cadaver of a contemporary tragedy, I thought, a provoked tragedy, a story of two mad people as mentally infirm as Octave and Armance. Theater tickets, that's what we are I thought. A tragedy of suspicion, of interpretation, idiomatic disturbances. Anguish in language. Sometimes English anguish, sometimes French.

They will live no matter where. The stubs of plane tickets: I keep. If I misplace them, I don't get upset about it. My religion is kind and moderate even in stubbornness.

"You have to help me, *Il faut m'aider*" – "*Médée?* Medea?" I say, do you remember?

– *M'aider?* or *tes dés?*[7]

– *Médée*, Medea, I say. New York. It was a long time ago. In Greek. – It was Handel's *Teseo*, you say. On the way out, you said to me: "**Many a thing do gods achieve against our hope**; that which we thought would be is not accomplished, while for the unexpected a god finds out a way." **A god breaks the way**.

– The same lines are found at the end of *Andromache*, *Helen*, *The Bacchantes*, *Alcestis*.

– We thought we were going to see *Medea* and it was *Andromache* do you remember? You're expecting Medea and it's Andromache I will never forget that switch. I have the tickets.

Look at this book of magic spells. Two theater tickets. We were in another century. It was 14.9.81. We sit down in the dark in two orchestra seats: this is the posture of initiates into the True Voyage. The sky opens, it changes kind. All of a sudden cities, we go by a hotel, we are in a room that we don't see and that feels as vast as the world. We are holding hands, an embrace full of thoughts of inseparation, it's a kind of admirable thought one has on the edge of a shore, hands are the whole bodies, a silent embrace, knowing full of thoughts that leave come back, each finger thinks about all the other fingers, one of those alliances that thinks tenderly, deliciously of death left outside. 14.9.81 a modestly mystical day with several worlds, we go from one world to another without awaking, without sleeping. The tickets recount what happened in the dark, in the delicacy of the secret, a long and slow event, mute metaphor of a life: a slow and long contact, with promise of a continent. A life: as if two legs wed each other for silence and for secret, as if in the crowd and among the restless

---

[7] The word play here is complex, between the homonyms *m'aider* and *Médée* and then *tes dés*, your dice, which lets one also hear *t'aider*, to help you. (Tr)

assembly of people, a leg loved a leg in a long and tender serenity, the calves like two does half-asleep flank to flank, in a long unhurried, unworried stroke, meditation of two legs on the confiding tone, does your leg remember? my leg remembers it was a long miraculous moment won, no one will ever speak of it, before this day of tickets, as if we had dreamed the same dream. I must have slept a hundred years by your leg. I woke up. Here is the proof of the dream. This is, you say in English – like all our true voyages from New York to Bordeaux from Toronto to Calcutta from Athens to Amsterdam, the most intense and intensely presently anachronistic (I translate).

The difference between the ticket and telling a story: the book of spells contains as well the trace of touchings, the mysterious memory of muscles.

Happiness of legs. The use of the body. This nourishing without ingesting, this response: the mouth must have its mouthful, the hand must have its hand, the leg must have its legful. The day after a day when I had wished for death, we were going to see *Medea*, it was *Andromache* and never had bodies known such gaiety. The evening before *Andromache* if I had been able to die, without that being either a figure of speech or an attempted murder, if I had been able to die without death and without killing, I would have wanted to die up against you but it's that very thing that is denied me, I spent the day wanting to stop loving you, at the worst of the pain I loved you against myself, I wanted to place my head on your shoulder, enter into your chest and double-lock myself in, "Mr Theseus put his hand on the Young Lady's shoulder exactly the way he put it on mine," I suffered, I would have liked to tear my shoulder off, having changed my person into a sacrificial beast, to cut its throat, but I was on the side of your shoulder and on the side of the Young Lady's shoulder, none of the aids that come to help, anger, indignation, revolt, incredulity, would ever come to my aid against you. You became a *he* and there was death in full daylight.

The next day I remember you quoted Euripides to me: "Many a thing do gods achieve against our hope; that which we thought would be is not accomplished, while for the unexpected a god finds out a way." We were driving at night, the theater was so far from Manhattan, countless the events that are achieved against our expectation, we think that for twenty years, without ever knowing if we are on the wrong side or the right side of love. Brooklyn Academy.

My religion is my invention. I ask no one to share it. The Cause is not in the blow. I tell you nothing about my practices. This is my natural way of life. My second nature. These various activities are the result of the complex form of my life with you. I should say: my lives. I have a life with your Presence and a life with your Absence that is another kind of presence. Your second Presence, in other words your Presence-in-your-Absence, your spiritual Presence commands the greater part of my active life. In-your-absence, that is to say your Presence with me in me, inside me, the world is entirely spiritualized, animated, impregnated with thoughts, I could say haunted by you, overhaunted, overexcited, it is made book and habitation, there is some spirit-of-you and the thing-of-you everywhere, in the bath towels as in the proofs of the book I am correcting. You have representatives of every sort: I have heavy water glasses peopled with bubbles that are you. Your poems are followed by a cortege of material sub-poems. I feel your blood pumping in the teapots, in the sleeves of my jackets, you are breathing in the shelves I meet you in the elevator whose mirrors keep a transparency of your image as you run through your hair the comb from the Hotel St George from which we could glimpse the Acropolis, the perspective was such that as you ran this comb through your hair I saw while looking at you in the glass of the large window the Acropolis form your crown in reflection, each time you take the elevator in the building, as soon as we enter the cage that belongs to our domain, you take out the comb from Athens, you smile at me in the mirror, you go down to the ground floor I go back up with your smile in the mirror at which I smile when I pass by one more time, the five hundredth? – the first time of the elevator we held one another intertwined you had your back to the mirror we formed the androgyne and together we thought of the adorable poem *Elevator* one of those that does not hurt me even if I would like to have been the one the poet embraces at the seventh floor – when I pass by one more time while smiling at your smile in the other world, that of images that live in mirrors and take shape again at our will. Lake Geneva for example. It keeps an image of you – perched on a rock and throwing not very far some bits of hard bread for the ducks, you have a serious air within the cleft of your gaze the thought, the color of the thought that I know so well and that murmurs "blessed be this instant of feeding the ducks of Lake Geneva that will never come back." And me, I keep the bit of paper napkin on which a little later in the café you wrote: ***still alive/ on lake shore twilight falls on 1990***. I thought: who is still alive? is it you alone, the still-living-always-a-little-dying one? is it us, is it love or the ducks or the twilight of the year, and still today I wonder who is speaking on the crêpe paper napkin from the café, I don't know how to translate **still alive** into French and neither do you.

To keep the Kleenex – it was enough to think of it. The rest is secret, silence, paper bags from Chanel Dior Rykiel

Thessie as well, called Messie, our witness, my heartbreak, the purest love of my whole life: kept. Thessie first of all and always at my side her cradle, snuggled up in her tallith, I will never move house again. What separates us is a nothing, a thin curtain of earth I place my hand on her right flank, I trace with my finger the extraordinary delicacy of her paws, I put my lips to the place where her head is and I cry torrential tears. On my lips in my hands flutters the absence of heat and the cold of our last nights, the tender warmth I spread over her and that she was good enough to accept so as to remain mine with me in her ultimate generosity. You are standing behind me August 30 returns I cry torrential tears, **still alive** you say we who are from now on the witnesses of our witness. – Further on, I say, beyond the end, love continues. – **There is a tongue in this skull** you say in your language. – Hamlet didn't put his lips to the lips of Yorick's skull, that is why he lost his life, I say. I would never accept that your skull be mixed up and abandoned. – You will go steal it and put it in a secret place.

Everything is language. I put my lips on the tiny mouth of our witness and I lick *her smile*.

You have to crouch to write the name and the chant of this day at the foot of the bookshelf in the bedroom, for the white-painted wall is almost full of inscriptions that sign our chronicle. Manuscript on wall. At first the author must stand on a stool, he writes a foot from the ceiling. Two years later, he is almost lying on his side. These body positions dictate forms and quantities, there are breaks in construction. Stylistically it makes for bizarre and powerful sentences. There is a tongue in this skull. If your readers only knew. Shakespeare, complete in five editions in English since my oldest book, *The Complete Works of William Shakespeare* **Oxford University Press Amen House London 1952 presented by the British Council 26.5.54**, first prize in English I was in Algiers, never left, what does it know? And fewer than ten years later, barely a minute in our play, next to complete Shakespeare next to *Todtnauberg*, next to the poor *Idiot* from childhood totally in tatters, your first collection, you had not yet been translated, **But never doubt I live**, I had not yet thought that you were alive in reality, one reads one thinks it's meant for no matter who for nobody for infinity you were already on my bookshelf among your peers, and now this book has spread, you are almost lying down on your side, you are writing yourself, and this is our last home, each sentence and each date increases the virtue of this apartment,

if one day I had to move but I will never move again, we would be nomads of the depths, here Olivier de Serres grows up everywhere.

From dream to dream, I try to return home, I have awakened in hundreds of different houses, one will be large, another underground, another full of holes, the April house was a delight, I phoned you come quickly. But where? It's on Rue du Monde, Street of the World. Look at the map. The number. I don't know. No one among us knows, we are all looking for it, my mother too, it has to be somewhere. All one would have to do is go down, look, but we are seeking feverishly for the interior exit door.

It's on returning to the bedroom of our fourth house after Olivier de Serres on Tuesday, June 1, 1991, that you said: but these words on the walls, these signs, this signature, someone could see them, who comes in here? I don't want to be indiscreet but who, I said who, you said: we have to hide this, I have to pencil it out, change the handwriting, I don't want them to see us naked, all at once you were gripped by fear that day, for years the bedroom had kept watch, why that Tuesday why that June, that day, that time? yes it's true it's I myself who wrote and signed and put my B and my I, we were looking at the large Bs all over the wall the dates were shining, put an O I say sadly put an N over the Bs and right before you left I said: do you want to put our No on your initials? No you say no, not today, we'll see, in twenty years, we'll see.

It's not easy to keep walls alive. But what about skulls? I am worried about my skull. Who will keep my skull who will keep your skull the way I keep our witness?

I am worried: who will keep the skull of the other?

Who keeps the best? The being who keeps or the being who forgets?

Artaud is worried about his skull. On 25.12.1940 he asks Genica to go look for it in the cemetery. You'll find it at Nanaqui he writes. "I am terrified by our resemblance" says the letter of 25.12.68, and here I am terrified by the word resemblance, to whom to relate it, to *us* who, to whom does *our* belong, terrifyingly. Between *our* and *resemblance*: a hole, in the hole: the poor skull of resemblance. We resemble one another like brothers, like brother and sister, like near and fear. Fear to see my old fear flushed out, unearthed and my skull barriers crack. In vain have I strutted around the city of poets, I am not yet altogether an atheist. Beware of the date. *"At year's end – Help the Post Office – Spread out your mailings."* Says the Post Office. Spread out your mailing. Please deposit Nanaqui's skull in the letter box. The skull is itself a box. Finally damned. Our resemblance took place from the first day to the last. Who will inherit our skulls? A question I had not asked myself before yesterday. I thought two nights ago I had a dream that led me to the Cemetery Library. As its name says it's the last Library. I went up to the large counter but without hope. The woman employee says to me: you are missing a letter, there. There was in fact a blank at the end of a line. I acknowledged it, but what to do? Where to find it? You had turned over these papers to me in this condition, and I didn't know to whom to turn for completion. Too bad, says the employee. With a *carné* [8] like that, she says you will not be able to access the rarest skulls in the library, because you are not really identified. What could I do about it? I was relegated, as usual. She turned over to me the small index volume of the library. I could see what I could aspire to and what was

---

[8] An adjective meaning meat-based or flesh-colored. The word one expects here is the homonym *carnet*, notebook. (Tr)

forbidden to me. I leafed through it. Each vestigial book was commented on in a few lines and evaluated as to its difficulty or its inaccessiblity. All of this is Dantesque. Certain volumes I saw bore the note: Joycean-Joycean, or Derridian-Derridian in Italian. The latter were designated the most ardent and unpronounceable. Me, with my missing letter, I would certainly have no right to them. I acknowledged a detachment of the retina. How to find our Resemblance or at least the resemblance of our Resemblance with this initial lacuna. In his last letter of horror Artaud asked Genica to be the resemblance of his heroine: "It's necessary to find the heroin(e) at all costs and it's necessary to get yourself killed in order to bring it to me here." That's where things were. Trust me, be calm. This letter was underlined by you. *To find the heroin(e) at all costs.*

I put up with animist joy because you exist and because I always have my placenta that brings me the orange juice that you don't bring me. The essential thing for living is that the secret be (1) well-balanced and well-managed (2) well-kept. I ask myself: would you have ever wished for a single life for two with cohabitation and conjunction? My laziness might be tempted. But my need to act and to create wants work and the fertilization of solitude. One can write only in the infinite interior desert with exits onto the passion bedroom. One can true-voyage only in great spasms, soaring, overflying abysses and continents. Why answer me on these questions? Everything I have just said is as false as it is true. I did not choose. I fell. The idea that my whole life was decided when I was twenty-three by a poem terrifies me. It's a truth with a Tibetan demon's smile and frown. It opens an equivocal mouth and says to me. "The good is *done*. The evil is *done*. Accept." It closes the equivocal mouth and it laughs.

I don't know if we live or if we escape death every twenty minutes.

To keep cities is another kind of concern, a very big deal. My great difficulty: everywhere that we have lived together the place has become ours. I cannot return there without him, without complications, without damages, without grief, without joys. The balance between the winds of passion is necessary but miraculous. I can no longer go to New York without him, I cannot not go there sometimes with him, sometimes without him. New York retains one of our lives that if we didn't go visit it would end up by drying out. We can't leave lives forever without re-lives. They are like dogs or cats faithful until death. They keep the City for us, with limitless generosity, what we forget from afar they keep intact in the meantime. Their power of memory is superhuman. But like everything alive our Cities of Lives need reincarnation. One has to go find them again sometimes. If not they become incredulous and finally phantoms. I don't know if it's the City that keeps one of our lives or if it's one of our lives that transforms the City into Enchanted City, into Theater in which are acted the scenes of our play, or if it's we who make for ourselves a City in our image. On Wednesday, October 20, 2004, we struck a double blow: I went to Montaigne while you went to Brooklyn, each one went without the other. We were in agreement you not being able to go to Brooklyn without me who goes to Montaigne for you. We got underway at the same moment, it was 8:00 A.M. it was 2:00 P.M., I was afraid that we couldn't leave after the stormy frenzy of the morning broken branches flood massive traffic jams one no longer knew which way, on both sides fear of going fear of not going where was I going, each time I make a pilgrimage there is a storm I am calling you from a downpour you say that does me good a sky on both sides, heavy swollen weather, the nervous sky, I cannot go to Montaigne sans your Spirit and sans your Body I say, what did you say speak louder, I scream into the telephone "Sans Your Body"; you scream "I sense it" we are screaming, in the wind Sense, Sans, I sense you, sans, in me I'm there, in the traffic, the rains, the years, how many years? all of a sudden those deserted streets and the funny little men with their crazy hats, so enigmatic – ten years ago already – ten or twelve? a little more a little less – where? – Williamsburg you remember Cabara that superb farm, its cloudy double in the water, and right here a crime – nobody anymore – what time is it? I am being looked at you say – I wonder why – little men – I have arrived, I say, I enter, are you coming? – a synagogue you say are you coming in? women are not allowed to come in I am not going in without you, I go-in-with-you, let's go in; here it's the universe – call it eternity if you want – what's lacking a little is time – I see Montaigne I say – I'm phoning you from the edge of his universe – but one can't deny we have something in common – 1 m 56 I would have preferred to spend my life with my ass in the saddle – and one can't not pray to someone either – transcendence – you say "transcendence" called the transcendental I say – it's no longer raining – I wait for everyone to leave the bedchamber – I'm at the prayer stool – I see it – the smallest temple in the world – room for one person with her or his interior other – get down on your knees – I hope that He hears you, you say – can you hear me? I say. I am calling you now from the bookstore, where are you? I say. – Lee Avenue, tell him that we will come back, you say, we will come back I say, to him.

But one can't always bring off a simultaneous translation. Sometimes there is some never-more in the air. We will come back you say. At that moment there's not a soul on Lee Avenue, and not a Jew, except us to come and come back, our faithful-forever phantoms

Lee you say and on my side I hear: *lis*, read.

IX

ON FEBRUARY 12,

I COMMITTED AN ERROR

LAST EPISODE

I had tried to commit this Error for the last ten years, its catastrophic phantasmagoria had presented itself to my mind at various times, and I had dismissed it too easily, as may happen when one plays at scaring oneself by imagining being led to make a mistake whose harmful consequences can be guessed at, so as to teach oneself a lesson or as it happens with me, and too often but I can't do anything about it, to represent to myself what I fear, that is to say the death of someone dear, with such an energetic scenario such striking images that I bewitch myself into a state of terror-by-probability or verisimilitude that is equal to reality. The fear that this imagined scene might be true overcomes me, a poison of despair spreads throughout my body, I don't move, I don't dare undertake to verify if my fear is real or if it remains confined in the horribly nearby realm of phantoms and nothing can undo the spell I have cast over myself, and which can take an altogether material form, except the apparition of the being whom I am in the process of dying out of fear of losing, in flesh and blood, on the garden path, quite alive and whose miraculous view brings me back to life.

I can do nothing against this mania of threatening myself which is a little crisis illness of my soul. So as to assume responsibility for it I've learned to use these morbid moments like firemen's exercises: since I can't prevent myself from being played with by fire, well, let these simulations be changed into maneuvers. Suppose there is a fire, and that one is ready to extinguish it. This fire would be perverse: one would have started it oneself. In the same manner each time, in past years, that I imagined myself causing my own ruin with an incurring act that is strangely called an *acte manqué*, I had seen the danger coming in imagination and I had sworn and sworn again never to let myself go near the edge of the cliff, a suicide happens so quickly.

Didn't I see the cliff coming that February 12?

Or else did I want it to come but behind my back, was I able to counter-wish for a feared accident?

Or had I pursued myself with wishes that were just as undesirable as they were desired much as one sees the chase between the Princess of Clèves and Nemours become more and more inexorable, good and evil having the same face?

We were not sitting on our divan, but on another, did this simple alteration in the setting of our intimacy suffice to unbalance my habitual resolution? The non-bedroom of our desert was not ours, it has more than once happened that we are in a borrowed place but with catlike quickness we have always reconstituted when traveling the eternal arrangement of our bodies in the habitual sky, me always sitting on your right, our knees slightly apart, the grazing of the knees caressing always furtively even when there is no one in the scene.

The date as well may have had its role. It is an anniversary date and one of great mourning for me. But we have always changed days of mourning into days of joy, our presence being the response *par excellence* of resurrection to misfortune. I am looking for neither an excuse nor a cause. I am depicting the circumstances and their incalculable ways of continuously turning upside down downside up.

I was thinking about life – thus about the death of my mother, with and without fear, nothing new because I think about that every day, I live on my mother, as on the earth, I live from my mother and in my mother who serves us as mother, nest, olive tree, because I consider every day as a day with her and without her as earth so I was thinking as I do every day about our death as the maternal chapter of our life, with and without fear knowing full well that what one expects is not accomplished, that our death would not be accomplished, and that it's an unforeseeable death that would be accomplished instead as always I was thinking about the upside and the downside of life, about the downside of the upside where we were, sitting on the divan, with the word divan opening slightly its Persian lips, we are at the *douane*, the custom-house I was telling you as-always, and I was thinking about the upside of the downside that we have always been.

You had just written your **Belated Answer to Celan**, you had just given me the *Answer*, I had it in my hands.

Celan, I thought, our non-witness.

"One is only through what one possesses" you were saying to me and "so many of our memories leave on journeys far from me, you were saying to me, I have millions of them, thus I lose millions of them I would have to have bodyguards, you are my true bodyguard." I have never forgotten your non-coming to Olivier de Serres and the events that followed, I was thinking. The "gods" who blaze a path for the unforeseeable are not more clairvoyant than the mortals over whose blindness their divine blindness throws a cover of clouds called destiny. No one saw anything. No one knows anything. Celan didn't ever know anything. My mother knows nothing.

Those who make the sky and the earth know nothing. You know nothing and you forget everything, I remember and I know nothing more. I had just written this book, I wonder if it is on the side of the upside or on the other side of the downside, I was thinking about the mystery of the book that is neither truly true nor truly false and that had ordered me to go back over our steps to look for the letters that were the authors of this incalculable total that is our being and that tell stories about us that we do not control. I am the guard of the true body, I thought, I keep everything, I write everything. I write the-book. I write the letters in the-book. The book sends me the letters. Am I inside – Am I outside? I have just given you this box of letters to read

And it's at that moment that I perhaps started out on the path toward the cliff.

When you began to recite our memory

what we do or don't do depends on the times as if we were reciting a *prayer*:

to make the resurrections return:

one time in bushes along the Marne river

one time at St John's College Oxford

one time at the Porte de la Chapelle station Paris

one time at Grand Central Station New York

one time at the Barrio Chino, the plane tree

one time – millions – you were saying, and for all the times that we found ourselves again together at the said place and time except one

– Do you remember at St George's Hospital after the News?

– I was sitting on the divan in 1990.

At that moment the telephone rang, I should have gotten up and answered but you answered: "The Police? It's a mistake." You came back and sat down. You said: "You attract the Police." It was the Police, I'm convinced of it. I should have taken this into account. – I was sitting on the divan. At that moment the telephone rang. The news was good. I fell on my knees.

In the darkness I didn't see the extremity of the cliff.

We did something we had never done, I said.

And there I should have stopped. I pricked up my ears. As if I could hear the edge of the cliff approaching. What were you going to say?

– We went to Kremlin-Bicêtre, you say.

To Kremlin-Bicêtre! Suddenly I bumped against the name of your forgetting. I stumbled. It was the moment to turn the lights back on. To change the subject.

At that moment, I committed the Error. I said: not Kremlin-Bicêtre. Bicêtre! I thought the word pained me. I said: Avenue de Choisy. Even then I should have turned left and run away, it would have been vitally prudent not to say "you said to me something there that you have never said in your whole existence," but I let fly that long, coarse sentence as if to hang myself from it.

– What?

I could no longer turn around to go back the cliff stood there and had a great simplicity. I was seized by panic: each step is a false step, *un faux pas*. I couldn't stop myself anymore. I tried not to go any further and I *saw* myself trying, it was miserable, it was two stories at once, in a noble version, in a vulgar version.

I heard myself saying: "I'm afraid to tell you," meager washed-out miserable words. "I can't" I was saying.

– Exactly, so tell me.

Now all of a sudden I didn't want to speak of it anymore, I didn't want to have spoken of it anymore, I didn't want you to come near the delicate and wavering beauty of my scene, I didn't want you to come near the prince of Avenue de Choisy whom I imagined you had perhaps been, the adored one that

I had perhaps procured for myself through fraud, through a false memory,

I couldn't say to you: "I'm afraid of you," that would have been to insult the one who you are and perhaps were not, "I'm afraid that you'll kill me, I'm afraid that you will destroy the silk of my story," I couldn't "I'm afraid you'll renounce the secret religion of my text," I couldn't say to you I'm terribly afraid of losing the most precious thing in the world (1) that you have forgotten you gave me (2) that you perhaps never gave me (3) that I possess alone and in secret (4) that I enjoy thanks to your phantom, what if I said it to you and then you say: me, I'm supposed to have said that? or: I've forgotten.

I was so afraid that I didn't know exactly what I was afraid of. My history, my phantom, my sublime scene my unique, what if you chased my thing away! No, I will not tell you, I say to myself.

I was afraid you would confiscate this moment, so brief and frail, thanks to which I have lived a crowned life, my very sweet and very fine improbable glory.

– Tell me

– Another time, I say. I was in despair. At disobeying you. I was gripped by bitter jealousy, but of what, of whom? It seems to me that I was jealous of the one that I had been until now.

I was on the point of surrendering the only witness of the Avenue de Choisy. The disavowal would be resounding. How happy I had been when I lived with the phantom of an event. I could tell myself whatever I liked, I did so, I had just done so.

I saw the moment of the abyss coming. The betrayal come from farther away had taken the secret path so as to enter into my interior temple and lay everything to waste.

No, I will not tell you.

And then I tell you.

What I say is very small.

I say: "you said the words '. . .'" and I murmured those two paltry words as if I were blaspheming, "it burns my tongue and palate without my having ever been able to know if you knew what you were doing." I say this sadly in embarrassment I confess a theft an indecency a very small great crime, I committed an Error and its double.

It's all my fault, I should have been silent but of the two of us you're the one who keeps silent me I keep Speaking and all wrong. I look at the ground, I don't dare look at you, I sense that if at this moment I phoned you out of the anguish of traveling it's someone other than you who would answer me. My gaze escaping from the cage that I myself have made runs to the back of the garden and stops before the piece of sacred ground to the left of the portal where Thessie our witness had elected her secret sojourn behind a spray of thujas when she lived outside my heart. But the hiding place is no longer, the thujas were torn out, the wall remains naked. Nowhere for Thessie to hide her shadow. The image of our witness hidden behind her trellis through which she used to watch us has no refuge anymore. And I myself am the one who in an act of violent inattentiveness ordered the removal of the thujas. I thought I was attacking networks of branches rotted by age. I caused the ruin of the trace. I said these cherished words that I'm not sure I did not dream and there is nothing left of them from now on except a withered breath expiring in the impermanent air. I lower my head, I look between my feet, all is nothing, I am dispossessed.

You get up. Sadly I take pleasure with an unspeakable sadness in feeling the power of nothings in the realm of Love, the need to take in my arms the being that I will never again be able to take in my arms plants its sharp little claws in my breast, tiny blessed bite of vain desire and I suck slowly the bitter powerlessness of love. Marvelous idiocy of my soul that undermines itself. You have gotten up. You say "come I am going to show you some photos." I get up, I go look at the photos. Your Egypt. We look at this Egypt for a long time. As if we were looking at the photos of the Gods. We do not see them. But they make their way in the mire. Were they already there on Avenue de Choisy in the acacias licking their lips saying to themselves: in ten years we'll get her?

Or else is that your Response? I wondered.

Or else you wanted to safeguard the unique mystery of Avenue de Choisy, the barbarian was me. I should therefore be delighted with your non-response that was in truth your response.

You said nothing. You got up. I still had your book to Celan **Belated Answer** in my hands. Time has no age for you I thought. Was I thinking in 2005 after J. C.? Were we not in 2005 before J. C.? Could it be Amon Re master of the Air and Fertility who arranged our unforeseen affairs?

Perhaps he will answer me in thirty years. This idea makes me laugh. Myself I had just received and non-received some letters dated forty years ago or almost. Some book letters. I saw us in thirty years. I was watching you as you put away the photos that is to say threw them like fistfuls of dust into a box. It was very dark. I took advantage of these very brief instants to note down my state in my pocket notebook. He is so strong and so fleeting. I note the fleeting. One can't imagine two more dissimilar beings. At that moment a storm took up the whole stage of the sky thundering for a long time with surprising uniformity then letting loose the first waters as if the master of water had opened wide all the sprinkler pipes up above. My thought followed the movement. One heard nothing anymore except this diluvian Speech, beautifully regular. Our little human words were put back in their place. You turned toward the window and you said something, but under the cannon roars it sounded like the murmur of a field mouse.

It seemed to me I heard something like "*Bon, on a ou*, once when it will be the last time the weather will be like this" or something like that. Naturally, I didn't say "what?" My voice too would have been swallowed up by the rain.

I am almost certain of having heard more or less the sentence I quoted. I said thank you silently to the Forces. One cannot say that you might have ordered the Storm. But if there had not been the Storm?

The Unhoped-for happens at the end of *Helen* at the last minute. There is no one left in the play. We have nothing else to do but listen to the Storm stronger than everything. You sat down beside me.

Now the Thing has been said, I thought. Now never again. There is nothing to be read on your face – its habitual gentleness.

One cannot listen again to the Unique Word. I will have to remember the Event. Am I going to forget it? Had you forgotten it?

Now all the years that come will be afters and never-agains.

"Did I hear what I heard? Do you think I heard?" If there had not been the accident of the Storm in which to slide words like a book into a worldwide letter box nothing would have happened

It's an Accident and all the same it's a wedding, I thought. And so late and so early.

I don't know what you're thinking. Your thought put your right hand on my left knee.

I don't want to forget, but I don't want to remember, I thought. But there is no master for forgetting or for remembering. When I return to my mother's, after the Storm, it is almost fully night, I am late because of the bad weather. She had waited for me to have dinner. The essential with the essential according to her. As for me I don't want to eat I want to think. I see that she has prepared some *Kartoffelpfannkuchen*. That means: "I love you" in the language of potatoes. When

I was little I adored these fritters made from raw grated pota-
toes. She says: I made some *Kartoffelpuffer*. I hope they're
still hot. I say: *Pfannkuchen*. She says: no: *Puffer*. No I say:
Pfannkuchen. She says: *Puffer*. She says: I didn't remember
anymore how they're made? It's been at least twenty years. I
say: you grate the potatoes, you strain them, you save the
starch. I recite the recipe of Omi my grandmother the mother
of my mother the mother of the fritters. Did one have to add
onion? says my mother. I say no. Paradise: with or without
onion? Sad paradise. My rose mother. I don't say a word.
Except *Pfannkuchen* and she: *Puffer*. The cats are dancing with
joy. The simple life lives. Life lives. I will never forget . . . says
my mother.